Mathematical Puzzlements

HERBERT KOHL

Mathematical Puzzlements

Play and Invention with Mathematics

SCHOCKEN BOOKS • New York

First published by Schocken Books 1987
10 9 8 7 6 5 4 3 2 1   87 88 89 90
Copyright © 1987 by Herbert Kohl

Library of Congress Cataloging-in-Publication Data
Kohl, Herbert R.
    Mathematical puzzlements.
    Bibliography: p.
    Includes index.
    1. Mathematical recreations. 2. Problem solving.
I. Title.
QA95.K55 1987   793.7′4   86–20430

Design by Jacqueline Schuman
Manufactured in the United States of America
ISBN 0–8052–4022–5

To Samuel J. Kohl, my father,
who first introduced me to
the magic of mathematics

� Contents ✄

4. Logic and Strategy   *165*

"You should learn not to make personal remarks," Alice said, with some severity; "it's very rude."

The Hatter opened his eyes very wide on hearing this; but all he *said* was, "Why is a raven like a writing-desk?"

"Come, we shall have some fun now!" thought Alice. "I'm glad they've begun asking riddles—I believe I can guess that," she added aloud.

"Do you mean that you think you can find out the answer to it?" said the March Hare.

"Exactly so," said Alice.

"Then you should say what you mean," the March Hare went on.

"I do," Alice hastily replied; "at least—at least I mean what I say—that's the same thing, you know."

"Not the same thing a bit!" said the Hatter. "Why, you might just as well say that 'I see what I eat' is the same thing as 'I eat what I see'!"

"You might just as well say," added the March Hare, "that 'I like what I get' is the same thing as 'I get what I like'!"

"You might just as well say," added the Dormouse, who seemed to be talking in his sleep, "that 'I breathe when I sleep' is the same thing as 'I sleep when I breathe'!"

"It *is* the same thing with you," said the Hatter, and here the conversation dropped, and the party sat silent for a minute, while Alice thought over all she could remember about ravens and writing-desks, which wasn't much.

—Lewis Carroll, *Alice's Adventures in Wonderland*

One thing ravens and writing desks have in common is that they both appear in *Alice's Adventures in Wonderland*. Here are a few more:

They both stand on their own feet.

They both start their lives in trees.

They both don't have propellers.

What does this all have to do with play and invention with mathematics? Everything. Self-reference—that is, the strategy of using the words "raven" and "writing desk" to solve a riddle about ravens and writing desks; the isolation and study of particular attributes, such as standing upright; the study of the emergence of different structures out of similar materials such as wood; and the use of negation as a method of proof are all mathematical techniques. And play, silliness, thinking the unthinkable are at the center of mathematical activity. Imagination is the central tool in the mathematician's kit.

This book is for people who like to think for the sake of thinking. It can be used to teach a course in mathematical thinking anywhere from junior high school to college. It can also be played with on the bus or train, and be a source of puzzlement that can ease the pain of traffic jams and airplane flights. I hope it contains challenges you will like to share with friends and with your children.

The best way to approach the material is probably to skim through the book and dip into an activity or puzzle that grabs your interest. Then you can go back and see how that specific challenge fits in the more general scheme of the section it's in. My idea was to give a reader the choice of going through a topic in some detail or just doing a puzzle or two in a spare moment. The main goal is to convey the magic of modern mathematical thinking in ordinary language, using challenges that require no previous experience with math. You do not have to have gotten good grades in school math to end up loving doing mathematics.

There are a number of people whose time, generosity, and mathematical sophistication have enriched this book. The first is Martin Gardner, whose writings on mathematical recreations I have read and played with since I was in high school and whom I have had the privilege to get to know in the last few years. Claudia Zaslavsky, a creative mathematician, a writer, and an exceptional teacher of mathematics, provided me with suggestions that have shaped this book. Joan Ross, a game designer, teacher, and mathematician, helped keep me honest by her wonderful critical reading of the manuscript. Claudia and Joan have also contributed to this book, and their help has been indispensable. The same goes for the editorial and personal support I've gotten from Pat Woodruff and the rest of the people at Schocken Books.

I'd also like to thank all of the people on the board of the now defunct Atari Institute for the irresistible and infectious pleasure they provided as we played abstract games in the crazy corners of the mind while trying to discover decent ways to use microcomputers. The Arena Press, Allan Nevin, Craig McMillan, and Judith Kohl did the illustrations and the stats that made it possible to make mathematical ideas visible in the text.

Finally, I owe thanks to my wife, Judy, and my daughters, Erica and Antonia, who put up with my bursting in at the most unlikely moments and imposing games and puzzles on them, and to my son, Joshua, who took time to test out many of the ideas in the manuscript and showed me how to structure this book.

Mathematical Puzzlements

An old French mathematician said, "A mathematical theory is not to be considered complete until you have made it so clear that you can explain it to the first person you meet on the street."

—David Hilbert

"Speak when you're spoken to!" the Queen sharply interrupted her.

"But if everybody obeyed that rule," said Alice, who was always ready for a little argument, "and if you only spoke when you were spoken to, and the other person always waited for you to begin, you see nobody would ever say anything, so that——"

"Ridiculous!" cried the Queen. "Why, don't you see, child——" Here she broke off with a frown, and, after thinking for a minute, suddenly changed the topic of conversation."

—Lewis Carroll, *Alice's Adventures in Wonderland*

Impertinent questions and sudden changes of topic are part of most of our lives. Sometimes these questions and the evasive responses they evoke are personal. Sometimes they're political. And sometimes they're mathematical. It is the mathematical impertinences—the puzzling questions about numbers and sizes and shapes, about infinity and eleven-dimensional space that occur to us in odd moments and to many children in even ones—that this book sets out to explore.

However, raising interesting questions is only a beginning. It is as much fun to invent or discover answers as to raise questions. It is not so much a matter of being right or wrong. Many of the puzzlements that occur to us have not yet been solved by any mathematician, and some may have no solutions. It is more that questioning and inventing keep the mind alive. The problem is how to develop the habit of doing mathematics. For most people, the experience of math in school is looked upon as bordering on the traumatic, and if you try to show them a mathematical puzzle or describe an interesting mathematical discovery, you're likely to get a response such as, "Oh, not me, I could never do math. Why don't you tell my cousin the accountant, who works with numbers every day."

Nevertheless, these same people can tell you the comparative price of food in a dozen supermarkets, do double acrostics with ease, recite sports facts and figures and make sophisticated predictions from them, play bridge or poker or dominoes, and manage to figure out how to plan and finance their vacations. They are mathematicians in their everyday lives and don't know it.

The same is true for children. When I was teaching elementary school, there were students who panicked every time they had to face a math test or worksheet. Yet they knew how to play craps, figure the betting odds on football and baseball pools, and calculate batting and earned-run averages, all of which demanded more sophisticated skills than the worksheets and tests imposed upon them in school.

Fear of mathematics is learned. I hope this book will contribute to the unlearning of this habit which deprives people of the pleasure that playing with mathematical ideas and puzzlements can provide. The book is not an attempt to duplicate the wonderful work that exists in the field of recreational mathematics. Martin Gardner's books, along with those of Raymond Smullyan, Douglas Hofstadter, A. K. Dewdney, John Conway, and others cited in the Recommended Reading section, are wonderful. My intention is to create a broader audience for them—to make more people feel that they can play with mathematics.

Learning to unlearn is an important and neglected aspect of growth. We all have dysfunctional habits. It is easy to develop feelings of inadequacy in the face of some challenges and avoid areas of life where we feel incompetent or have experienced failure. Conscious unlearning requires letting go of the fear of failing and, in private if necessary, playing with no goal in mind other than to explore an aspect of experience that was previously inaccessible. It is a form of escaping testing, grading, and all forms of categorization. It is also learning to enrich life by unlearning the feeling of being put down. In the case of mathematics, it means playing without a teacher to judge you and not worrying about the right answers so much as working to understand the questions.

The puzzlements in this book are meant to encourage exploration, and though many of them should amuse and challenge experienced mathematical gamesters, most provide the reluctant mathematician or puzzler with puzzlements ranging from simple to sophisticated and complex. The answers to the puzzlements are themselves explorations of problem-solving strategies, structures of proofs, and ways of raising new questions. They are meant to introduce you to playing with math the way you might learn to play guitar or piano or softball. Skills develop, mistakes are inevitable, personal style is essential, and the goal is taking pleasure in the workings of one's own mind. For that reason, I've concentrated heavily on activities you can do as well as puzzles you can solve, on pattern making, graph sketching, and paper-and-pencil games. The tools you'll need to play with the puzzlements are paper, a set of colored pencils, a good eraser, a pair of scissors, and an active mind. That's usually what you'll find in every mathematician's tool kit.

But why puzzlements instead of puzzles? A puzzlement is not an individual puzzle or even a collection of puzzles. It is a question that pushes the limits of ordinary thinking and can be illuminated by puzzles, paradoxes, diagrams, games, and even apparent contradictions. Here are a few: Does 2 + 2 always have to equal 4? Is it possible for parallel lines to meet at infinity? How does game strategy change if the object is to lose instead of to win? What would life be like in two or twelve dimensions, or on the surface of a doughnut?

There are no set answers to these questions, though there are many puzzles and games that illuminate them. Doing mathematics is not always a matter of getting correct answers. I want to provide people who are not mathematicians with the experience of playing with ideas about shape, position, size, process, and structure—these constitute the central concerns of mathematical thought.

If we were taught mathematical thinking in school rather than just calculating, re-proving other people's theorems, and solving equations, the wildness and beauty of mathematics would be more widely appreciated. We would be able to do mathematics just as we listen to music—by choice and according to our tastes and time.

The reason I've written this book is that when I was in high school I had a math teacher, Louis Cohen, who laughed and jumped up and down when he explained how to solve a math problem. He called solutions beautiful, ideas elegant, and used the language of literature, art, and music to describe mathematics. It was a revelation to me. Before that, math was simply something one had to do in order to get into college. I would like to share his love of mathematics and convey some of the joy and energy that the play of the imagination in the world of mathematics can provide.

Patterns on the Plane

A mathematician, like a painter or a poet, is a maker of patterns.
—G. H. Hardy, *A Mathematician's Apology*

If triangles had a god, he would have three sides.
—Montesquieu, *The Persian Letters*

If you take a look about, you'll find patterns everywhere in nature and culture. At this moment I'm sitting on a chair with a woven seat. The rug on my floor has mats created out of squares sewn together. My sweater has a striped weaving pattern and my shirt is checkered. The pillows on my couch alternate stripes and checks. There is a grainy pattern on my wooden desk, and the hi-fi speakers are covered with a mesh made out of tiny hexagons. The grooves on the records seem to make a circular pattern, but I know they have to be part of a great spiral or else the needle would be caught in an endless groove. Outside the window I can see the branch patterns of fir and oak trees, and the grooves cut in a hillside by a small stream.

Usually I don't pay particular attention to all these specific patterns that are part of my everyday life. But compiling materials on the mathematics of patterns has made me much more aware of the presence of pattern and of how mathematics often plays with the familiar in unfamiliar ways.

In this section I'll introduce some of those ways and present recreational challenges and experiments. The material is drawn from different areas of mathematics, such as topology and combinatorial geometry. However, you don't need any background in these fields to understand and play with the material. Most creative mathematicians don't pay much attention to field boundaries anyway. They approach subjects and problems that interest them from as many different directions as seems useful.

The language of pattern, the tiling of a surface, and the creation of interesting designs are activities that involve the visual element in mathematical thinking yet don't feel like school math. Play around with the designs and patterns, create your own material, and feel free to think that you're not doing mathematics, but just having fun.

Tilings and Tessellations

The two-dimensional geometric plane stretches off to infinity in two directions that can be thought of as horizontal and vertical. It can be thought of as a wall with no thickness; an imaginary slice through the universe. That wall can be tiled with repeating forms just as we tile our thick, finite walls with wallpaper and our floors with patterned linoleum. On our floors and walls, however, there is always an end to the surface and so at the corners we sometimes have to cut the paper or tile in the midst of a repeat of the pattern. In mathematical tiling, which we'll play with here, there is no end to the repeats of the pattern either horizontally or vertically. Try to keep that in mind when you experiment with your own tiling patterns.

Tessellations are special kinds of tiling and provide a nice, simple palette for the exploration of patterned ways of dividing the plane. *A tessellation is a complete covering of the plane by repetitions of the same shape.* The shape can be rotated, reflected (flipped over so that, for example, both

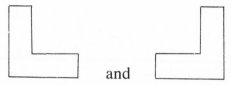

can be used in a tessellation), and shifted. Here's an example of shifting:

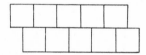

There are an infinite number of shapes that will tessellate the plane. However, the Greeks proved that there are only three *regular* shapes (shapes whose sides are all the same length and whose angles are all equal) that will tessellate the plane. They are the equilateral triangle, the square, and the six-sided hexagon. Here are simple examples of what these three tessellations look like unadorned. Notice that the shapes that go over the edges of the frame are cut off. You should imagine the tiling spilling over these edges and going on forever.

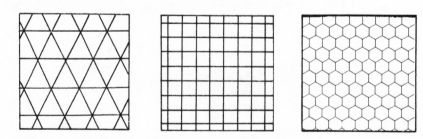

There are many ways to combine and modify these shapes to create interesting tessellations. You can reproduce the grids on pp. 25–26 and use them to create your own tessellations. Let's start by playing with the equilateral triangle.

Triangle Tessellations

The equilateral triangle has three equal sides. Each of its angles measures sixty degrees. If you put one equilateral triangle above another, you get a diamond. The basic equilateral triangle tessellation can also be seen as a diamond tessellation, as the following diagram shows:

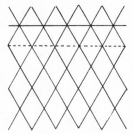

If you put six equilateral triangles together, you get a hexagon, so equilateral triangles can also lead to hexagon tessellations:

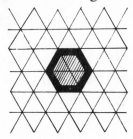

It is easy to transform a tessellated grid into an interesting patterned design by coloring in some of the shapes. Here are some examples using black and white. With a set of colored pencils, you can design many more triangulated patterns. When you try, imagine that you are creating wallpaper, cloth, or tiles.

Here are two more simple triangle tessellations:

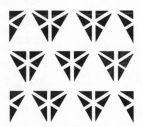

Now try shifting colored triangles:

Notice how the overall pattern changes. The shift creates a certain disorder that frequently makes patterns look more interesting. You can shift any distance and maintain the tessellation as long as you do it regularly and consistently.

Here is a fabric design that uses a triangular tessellation in an interesting way. The pattern depends upon the alternation of stripes created by rotating the basic triangle 180 degrees and making a diamond out of the original and the rotated form. In fact, any triangular tessellation can also be looked at as a diamond tessellation, and some, such as the one below, are constructed out of diamonds that cannot be broken down into triangles, because they are not symmetric.

In the following figure, there are systematic breaks in the diamond pattern so that part of each diamond spills over into another one. It's quite easy to learn how to do this, and it makes the tessellations you create much more interesting.

Here is another diamond tessellation. The basic diamond unit is outlined in the upper left corner.

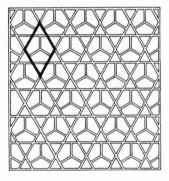

In triangular tessellation, the triangles fit together like puzzle pieces, some facing up and some facing down.

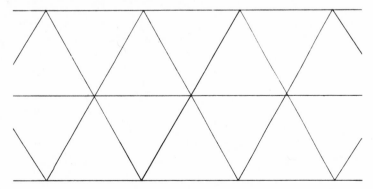

Because of the way the triangles fit together, you have to pay particular attention to how modified triangles look when they are flipped over (flips are permitted when you make tessellations). When you make a change on the left side of one triangle, you also automatically make a change on the right side of the flip of that triangle.

1 and 2 are the flips of each other

To make your own triangular tessellations, start with a strip of triangles and decide what you want to do with them. Remember that you can shift and flip the patterns, so it makes sense to pay attention to how your modified triangle will look when you turn it over.

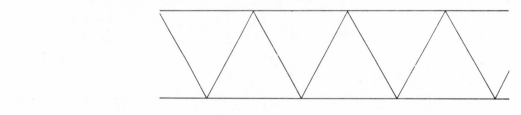

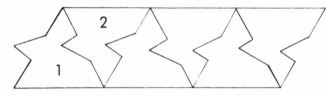 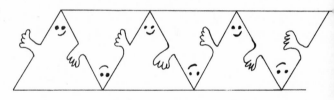

Here are some other modifications of the triangle:

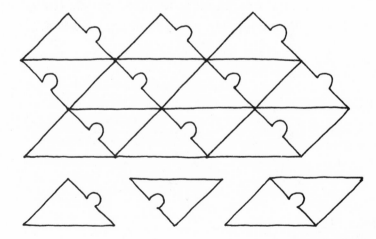

Try many different variations of your basic idea. The only thing to bear in mind is that, to maintain the tessellation, every triangle has to be changed in the same way. However, if you prefer art to tessellation, you might want to vary the pattern in some of the triangles so that there is some irregularity and perhaps mystery in the final work.

Square Tessellations and Deformations of the Square

Here are some textiles that use square or rectangular tessellating patterns:

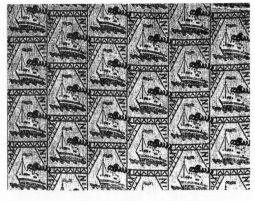

Begin with a block of squares such as this one:

Then modify one square and see how the modification affects the other ones. When you do this, you have created a new tile that will tessellate the plane. It is a good idea to draw that unit tile and then try to play with patterns within that tile:

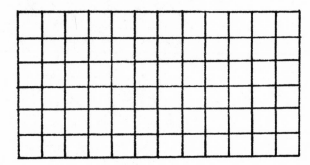

new tile:

Below are a number of modifications of the square that might give you ideas for your own tiling patterns:

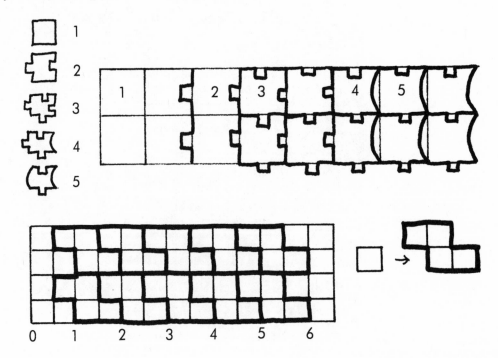

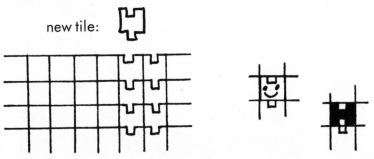

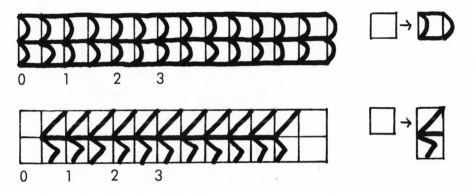

It is also possible to break a square, rectangle, or other parallelogram* down into smaller units and create patterns within patterns:

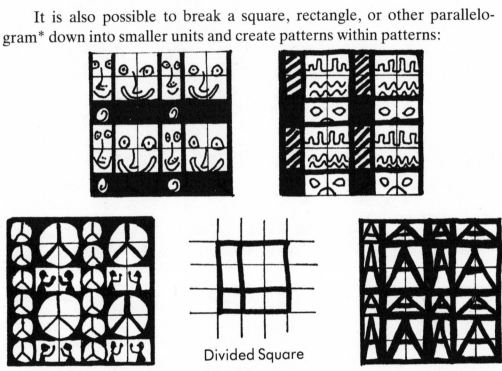

Divided Square

The square is not a rigid form like a triangle. Therefore, if you have a tessellation of squares, you can bend and stretch them into other parallelograms and still tessellate the plane:

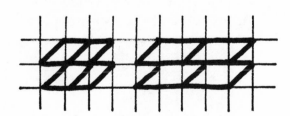

*A four-sided figure whose opposite sides are parallel: ▱ ═ ╱ ╱

Here's another example. Notice that the basic flag 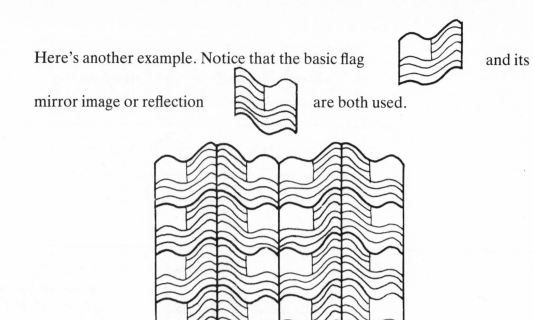 and its mirror image or reflection are both used.

There is a simple geometric property that makes it easy to tessellate the plane with any triangle by using it and its flipped version. Every triangle can be seen as half of a parallelogram:

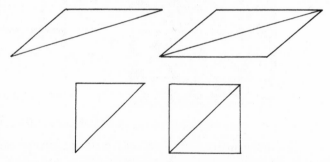

Using this insight, by creating a series of parallelograms out of any given triangle, you can get a simple tessellation of the plane. A little design ingenuity—and interesting patterns emerge:

There are also ways to tile the plane by using squares of different sizes:

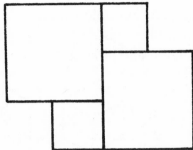

Here's a sample of a textile pattern using this kind of tiling:

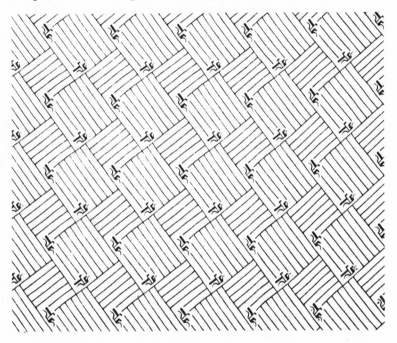

It's also possible to fill the plane with a number of differently patterned squares that end up creating an overall pattern:

Hexagon Tessellations

The hexagon is the third regular polygon that tessellates the plane. One interesting feature of the hexagon is that it can be divided in a number of ways. For example, it can be made to look like various views of a cube. It can also be divided into six equilateral triangles, a rectangle and two triangles, and other geometric forms:

Through coloring and drawing, hexagonal tessellations can be turned into what look like three-dimensional tilings of the plane:

Below are some more hexagon tilings. Notice how you can build interesting forms if you start with a hexagonal grid and then erase the borders or connect patterns across them.

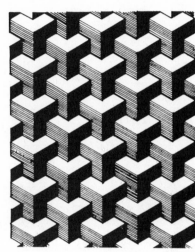

Mixed Tilings

Below are a number of what could be called mixed tilings—that is, tilings that use more than one shape.

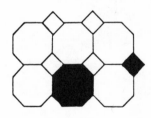

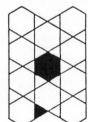

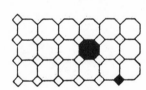

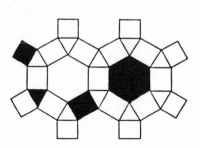

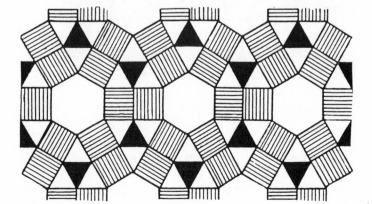

Tilings and Tessellations

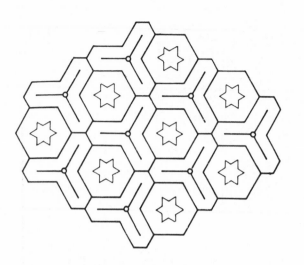

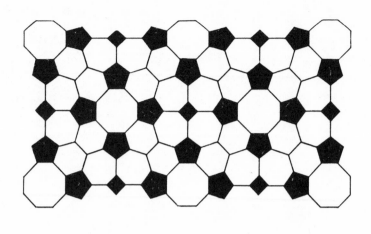

The Tessellations and Tilings of M. C. Escher

The Dutch artist M. C. Escher was a master of using tessellations and tilings. Here are some examples of his work.* Try to pick out the basic units. One way to do it is to trace over what you think are the central design units and see if, by repeated tracing, you generate the whole design.

*From M. C. Escher and J. C. Locher, *The World of M. C. Escher* (New York: Harry Abrams, 1972).

Here are some hints on how to make Escher-type tessellations. They are taken from the brilliant book *Handbook of Regular Patterns: An Introduction to Symmetry in Two Dimensions,* by Peter S. Stevens (Cambridge, Mass.: MIT Press, 1981). Anyone who wants to play with pattern and design should buy or borrow a copy.

You can develop Escher-like patterns in a straightforward manner. Simply interconnect with a single line any three corners of a parallelogram. Figure 1 gives an example. You can then alternate horizontal bands composed of direct renderings (translations) of the line with horizontal bands composed of mirror images of the line. Additional refinement produces the high-steppers of figure 2.

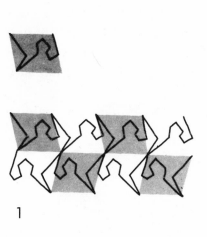

1

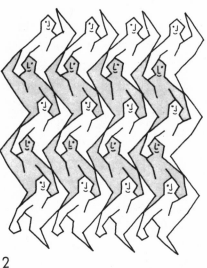

2

Here is a slightly more difficult analysis:

3

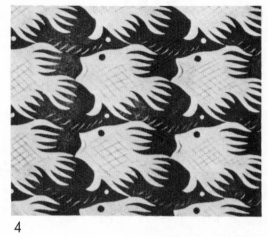

4

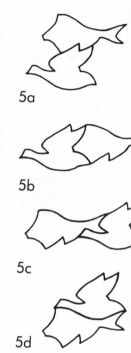

5a

5b

5c

5d

In figures 3 and 4, the *fundamental region* consists of a bird combined with a fish. The unit cell is a parallelogram in figure 3 and a rectangle in figure 4. Figure 5 shows four different fundamental regions for the design of figure 3, that is, four different ways to combine the bird and fish to make a single piece that can join with itself to fill the plane.

Trace a cut-out and make several copies of 5a to 5d. Piece them together to see how these fundamental regions fill the plane.

How difficult is the creation of such interlocking patterns? Probably both easier and more difficult than you imagine. It is easy to obtain a pattern made from a single interlocking piece, but difficult to develop the piece so that it looks like a natural form. To draw a piece that interlocks with itself, start with a parallelogram (a square or rectangle is permitted) and modify opposite sides in exactly the same way. You add to the bottom the area taken from the top, and to the left side you add the area taken from the right side.

The resulting piece is a fundamental region which will fit with itself to fill the plane without gaps or overlaps.

Patterns on the Plane

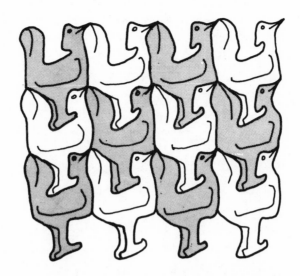

Using these tips given by Peter Stevens, create your own fundamental regions. For additional suggestions, turn to the discussion of symmetry on pp. 62–72.

Here are three grids for making your own tessellations and tilings.

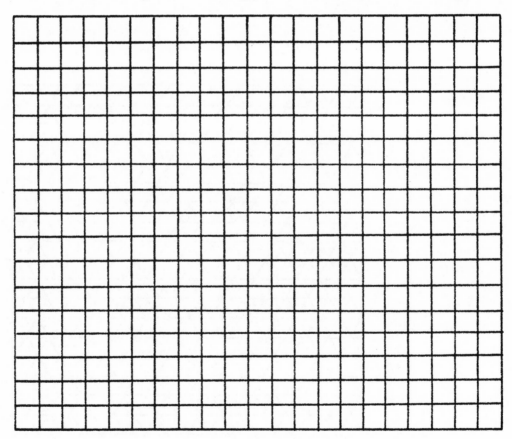

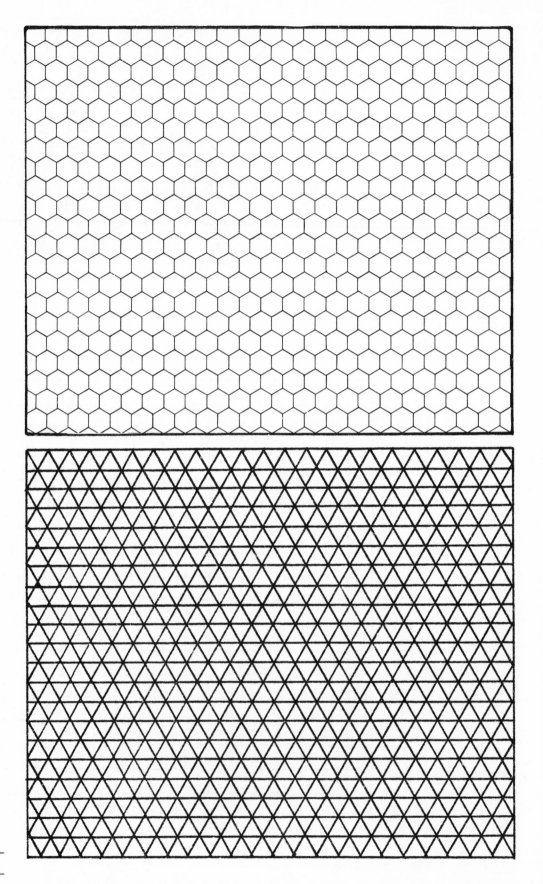

Patterns on the Plane

Rep-Tiles

Solomon W. Golomb, who teaches engineering and mathematics at the University of Southern California, pointed out a certain class of irregular polygons that tessellate the plane. These figures can be divided into other figures that duplicate themselves. For example, the trapezoid below on the left is divided into other trapezoids that duplicate it on a smaller scale. They in turn can be divided and their parts divided, etc. He called the self-modeling shapes Rep-Tiles. Here are three Rep-Tiles. Try to divide them into parts that fill them up and duplicate the original shape. Then play around with discovering other Rep-Tiles.

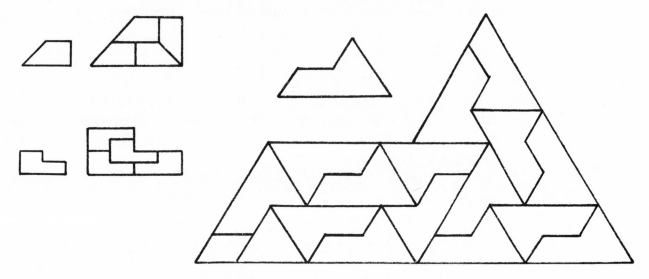

Polyominoes

Many mathematicians enjoy relaxing over a game of chess, checkers, or dominoes. However, the mathematical mind is a restless one, and even a simple game like dominoes can become the basis of abstract speculation and theory building. Solomon Golomb raised the game of dominoes to the nth degree and made it the subject of mathematical speculation in his book *Polyominoes* (New York: Scribner's, 1965). He begins with a one-unit square, the monomino:

All the rest of Golomb's polyominoes are built up out of combinations of this square.

It is magical to study the way in which an elegant and complex system emerges from this simple beginning. Golomb's polyominoes, in fact, impressed science-fiction writer Arthur Clarke so much that he used them as the building blocks of his universe in the book *Imperial Earth*.

A domino consists of two squares joined along one of each of their edges. There is only one domino shape:

Two squares that meet at a corner, or at edges that do not coincide, are not considered legitimate dominoes. These are not dominoes:

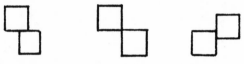

Golomb generalized the notion of domino and considered the properties of triominoes, tetrominoes, pentominoes, and in general *n*-ominoes where *n* stands for any integer and an *n*-omino consists of *n* unit squares joined along their edges.

A triomino, for example, is a tile formed by joining three squares edge to edge:

Here is another possible triomino:

Notice that 3 is the mirror image of 2:

For Golomb, all -ominoes that are mirror images of each other are considered to be *equivalent*. What this means in terms of the games and challenges involved with polyominoes is that you can always flip over an -omino in order to solve a problem.

Fill up this rectangle using triomino 2:

A simple solution involves flipping 2 to 3 once:

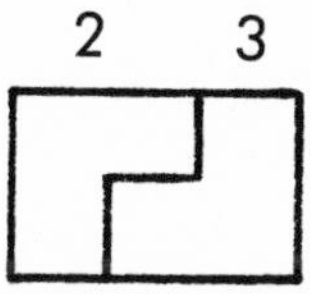

Golomb also considers all rotations of the same -omino as identical. Thus, in the case of triominoes, all of these rotations of 2 are considered identical:

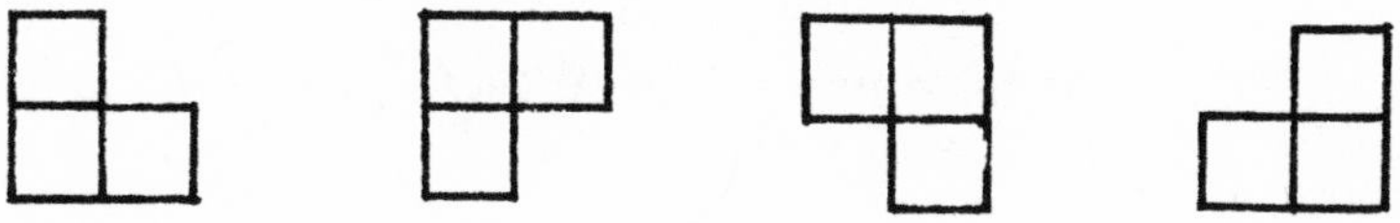

Remember when forming sets of -ominoes and solving puzzles that mirror images and rotations of a given -omino are considered identical! This being so, then there are only two triominoes:

Make a set of eight triominoes for yourself (four of type 1 and four of type 2) and try to solve these challenges:

Fill up the following figures with triominoes, leaving no empty spaces. There is more than one way to solve each challenge. Try to find as many as you can. Also see if you can fill up the grid using only one kind of triomino (you can use more than one of each triomino, and of course you can flip the triomino 2 over whenever you like).

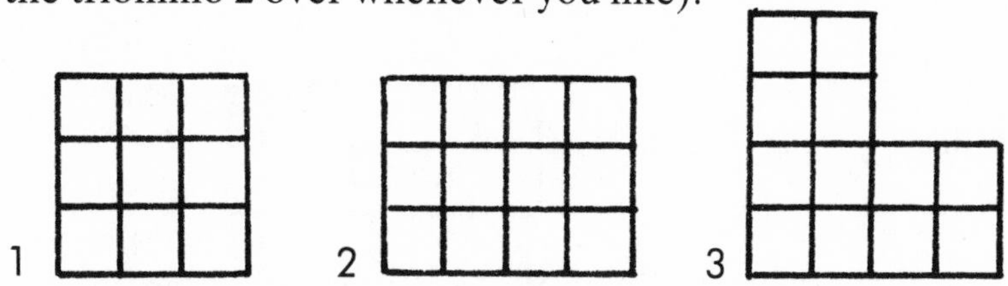

1   2   3

Solutions:

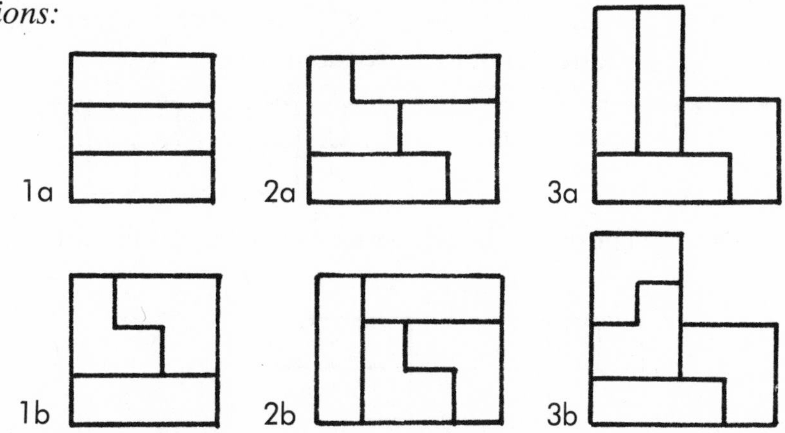

1a   2a   3a

1b   2b   3b

single unit size

These are not the only solutions to some of the problems. Try to discover others or, if you can't, try to prove to your satisfaction that there can't *be* others. Also, when you think you've found all the solutions to a particular challenge, try to reason out why your solutions are exhaustive. These simple exercises in informal proof construction will help you get a feel for how mathematicians explore new fields and problems.

Now try to fill up the following figures with triominoes. You'll find the task impossible. Why?

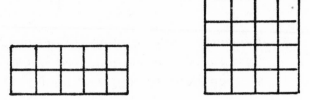

Answer: Triominoes can only fill a grid in which the number of squares is evenly divisible by three. By removing squares from the grid, the task becomes manageable. Try these modified grids:

Solutions:

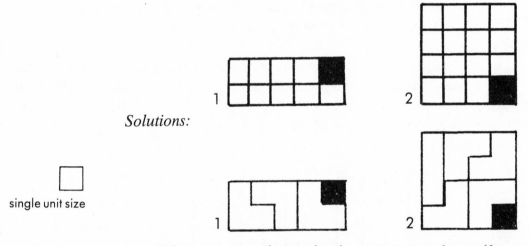

single unit size

When we move from triominoes to tetrominoes (four squares joined along shared edges) the level of complexity increases significantly. Here is a set of the five possible tetrominoes (remember that mirror-image and rotated -ominoes are identical):

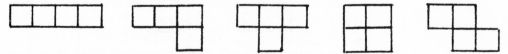

These are the tetrominoes that have mirror images:

Patterns on the Plane

Cut out four unit squares and try to combine them along their edges in all possible ways to convince yourself that there are no combinations that have been left out of the set given here. Also build that same set out of triominoes. Doing this will give you a proof that you have generated all the possible tetrominoes.

To make pentominoes (five units), begin with one of the five possible tetrominoes, say, this one:

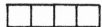

Add squares to it along all of its edges, like this:

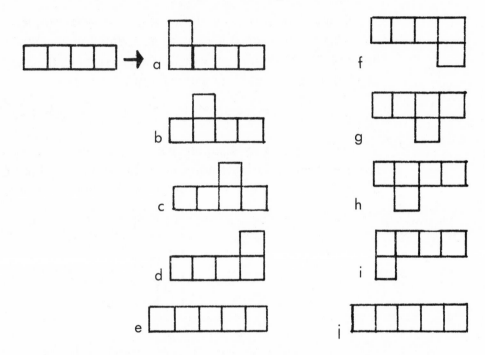

Now consider which of the pentominoes generated this way are mirror images of each other or which are identical if you rotate them in the plane (like the one below), and throw out all but one of them.

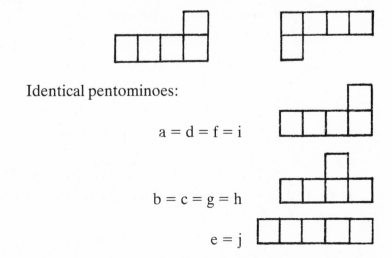

Identical pentominoes:

a = d = f = i

b = c = g = h

e = j

This results in a partial set of pentominoes:

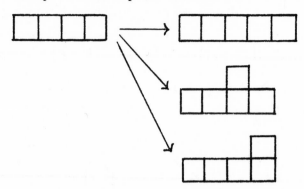

Repeat the process with the other four tetrominoes.

Join the five sets you constructed, and you have all the possible pentominoes. There is no other way that a new one can be generated, since every pentomino has to contain within itself a tetromino.

Make several sets of tetrominoes for yourself and try these challenges:

Fill up this 4-by-4 square with four identical tetrominoes. (This task requires four sets of tetrominoes). You should be able to do this in at least five different ways and with four of the five possible tetrominoes.

Solutions:

single unit size

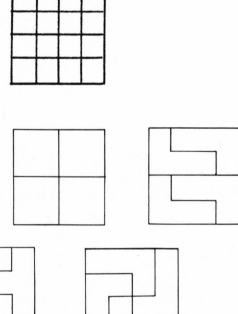

See how many different tetrominoes you can use to fill up this 4-by-6 grid. You can choose any number of identical tetrominoes and use any combination of different ones.

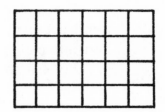

Solutions:

There are two ways to do this. The first uses three different tetrominoes, the second four different ones. (Remember that in all of these challenges there is more than one way to solve the problem. If you come up with a solution that is not in the book, don't worry: the solution is the answer. You don't need a book or expert to tell you that you're right.)

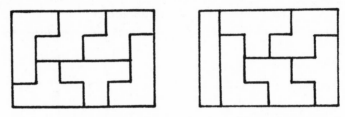

Fill up this grid with four identical tetrominoes. Try to do it in at least three ways.

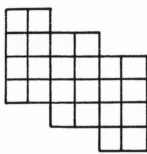

Solutions:

Here are three answers (there may be more!). Try to find more, and if you find that one tetromino can't fill up the grid, prove to your satisfaction that it is impossible to do. Impossibility proofs are major elements of the mathematician's tool kit.

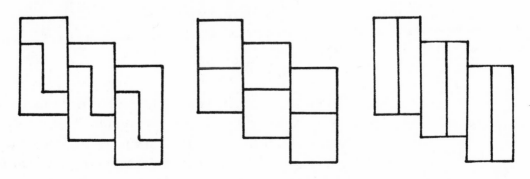

If you play around with the tetrominoes a bit, you'll find that you can construct many different and interesting shapes which you can trace and turn into puzzle challenges for your friends.

For example, this construction:

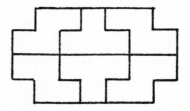

can be turned into this challenge:

Fill up this grid by using at least two different tetrominoes. You can use more than one of each kind.

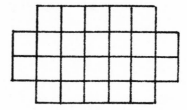

Now for the most popular set of -ominoes, the pentominoes:

single unit size

Here are the eight pentominoes that have nonidentical mirror images. Remember that in solving pentomino challenges you can use a pentomino and its mirror image (which you get by flipping a pentomino over). You can also rotate pentominoes. This makes for a nice visual fluidity in creating and solving pentomino puzzlements.

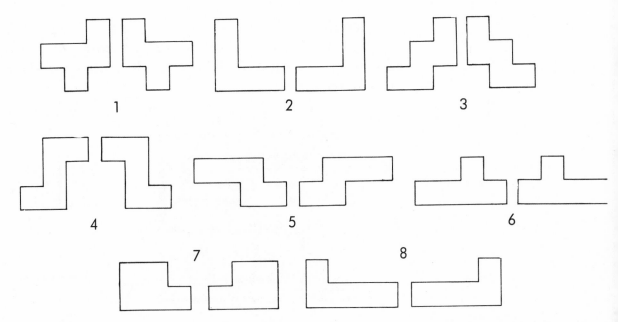

There are twelve possible pentominoes (look at the entire set in the illustration on p. 34). You can make several sets of pentominoes yourself or buy one at your local toy store. Golomb used pentominoes to create a very interesting and popular game of that name which is readily available in most toy stores. It is played on a chessboard whose squares are the same size as the squares that form the pentominoes. The game is a delight to play, and it also familiarizes you with the range of pentominoes, making it easier to solve pentomino challenges.

The twelve pentominoes are placed on the table next to the board. Two players take turns in picking a pentomino and placing it on the board. Play continues until one player has no place to put a remaining pentomino or until the board is completely covered by all twelve pentominoes. The player who is left with no move loses.

Pentomino games are very short and yet require ingenuity and experience. Here is a game in process:

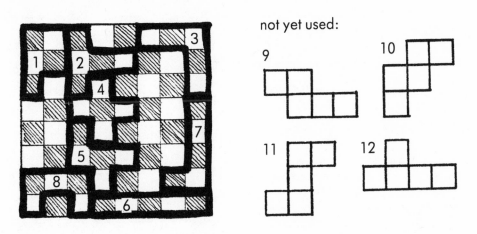

not yet used:

Another version of the game involves placing pieces edge to edge on the board and building a single shape. The goal is the same as the regular game: to have the last possible move. Here's an illustration of this version of Pentominoes:

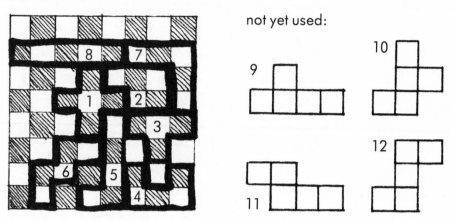

not yet used:

Here are some more pentomino challenges, several of which were suggested to me by Martin Gardner:

Build each of these figures out of two pentominoes that are equivalent to each other (that is, are either mirror images or rotations of each other). There is more than one way to do each of the challenges.

single unit size

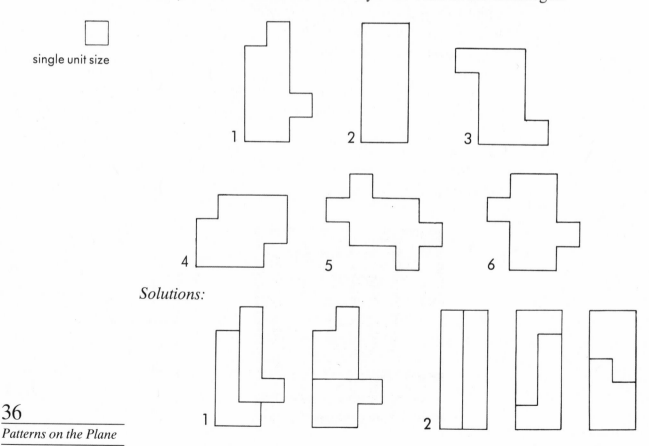

Solutions:

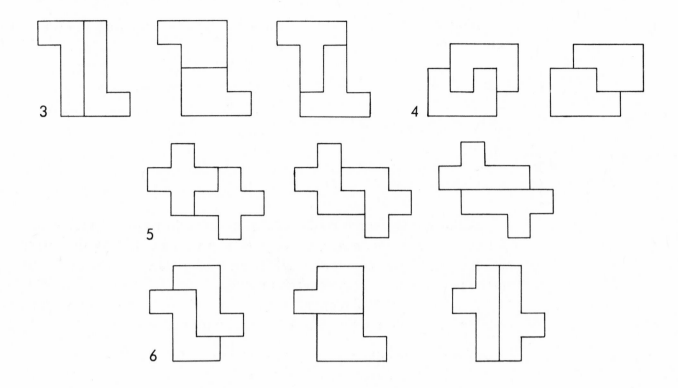

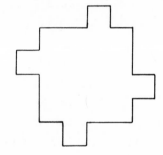

Find four different ways to fill this shape with four equivalent pentominoes:

Solutions:

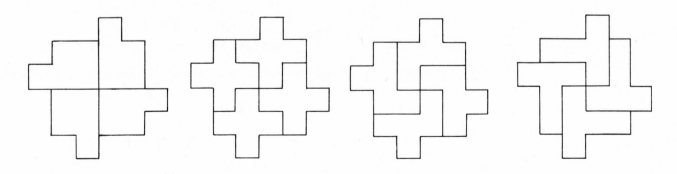

Find two different ways to fill up this cross with four equivalent pentominoes:

Solutions:

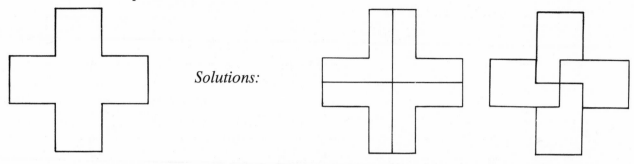

Following are some challenges taken from Lorraine Mottershead's *Sources of Mathematical Discovery* (Oxford: Basil Blackwell, 1978), which should be a resource for all teachers who want to present mathematics in a way that will delight their pupils.

Draw the specified rectangles on a piece of graph paper and then try to fill them completely with the designated pentominoes:

3 × 5 rectangle	any 3 pieces
4 × 5 rectangle	4 pieces
2 × 10 rectangle	4 pieces
5 × 5 rectangle	5 pieces
3 × 10 rectangle	6 pieces
7 × 5 rectangle	7 pieces
4 × 10 rectangle	8 pieces
9 × 5 rectangle	9 pieces
10 × 5 rectangle	10 pieces
11 × 5 rectangle	11 pieces
10 × 6 rectangle	all 12 pieces

(It is possible to arrange them in such a way that each pentomino touches the border of the rectangle.) Don't give up! There are 2,339 ways of doing this.

12 × 5 rectangle	all pieces (1,010 ways)
15 × 4 rectangle	all pieces (368 ways)
20 × 3 rectangle	all pieces (2 ways only)

Color each completed rectangle, using no more than four colors.

Solutions:

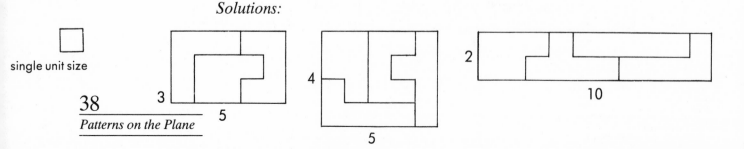

single unit size

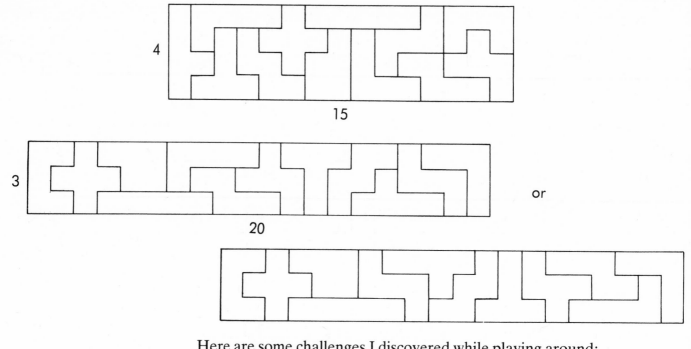

Here are some challenges I discovered while playing around:

Make this head with all twelve pentominoes, using each one only once:

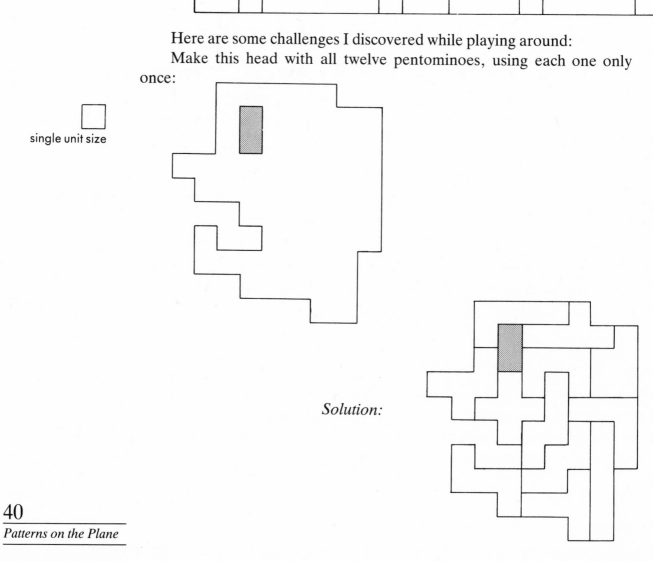

single unit size

Solution:

Make this dog, using six pentominoes:

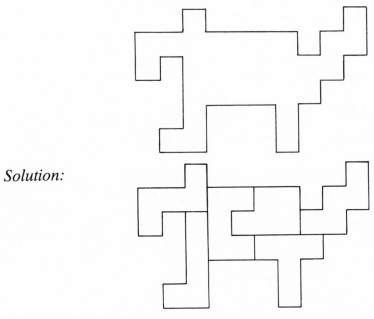

Solution:

Try to make this man out of the whole set of pentominoes:

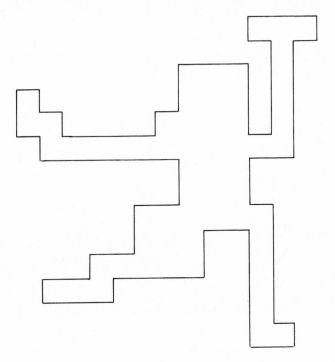

Solution:

single unit size

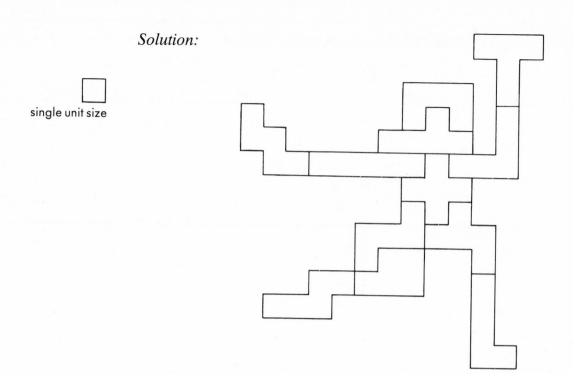

Try to build this fleet of ships out of the whole set of pentominoes:

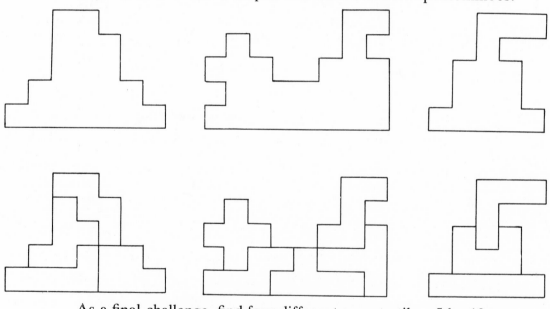

As a final challenge, find four different ways to tile a 5-by-10 rectangle using ten pentominoes.

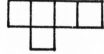

Solutions:

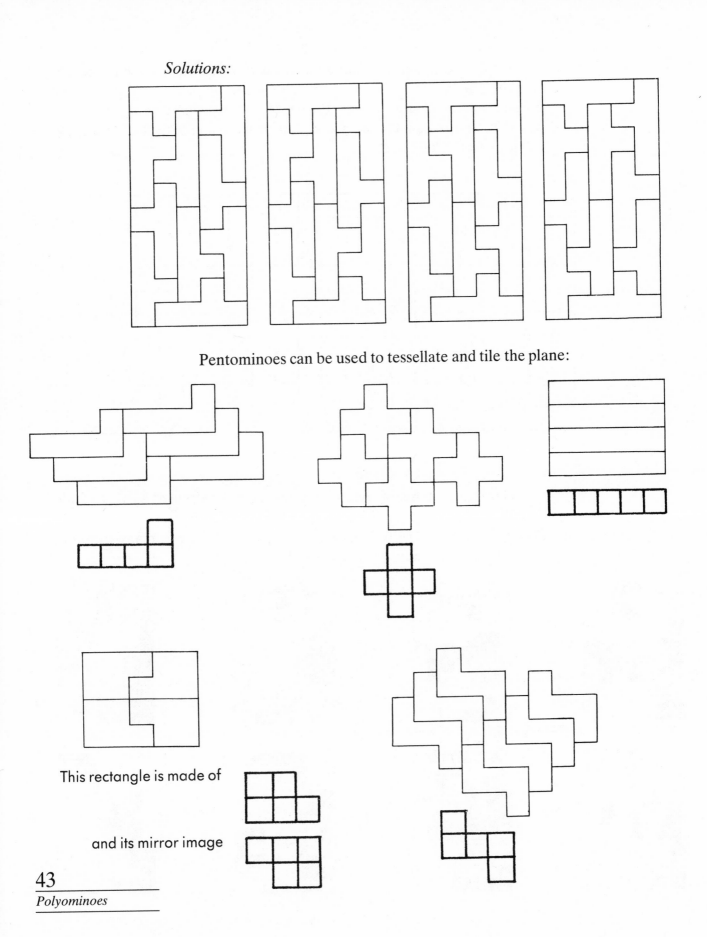

Pentominoes can be used to tessellate and tile the plane:

This rectangle is made of

and its mirror image

Explore for yourself whether every pentomino can be used to tessellate the plane. The whole set can, since it can be pieced together into a 5-by-12 rectangle and, as was illustrated in the section on tessellations, any rectangle tessellates the plane. This is what one such pentomino tessellation would look like:

single unit size

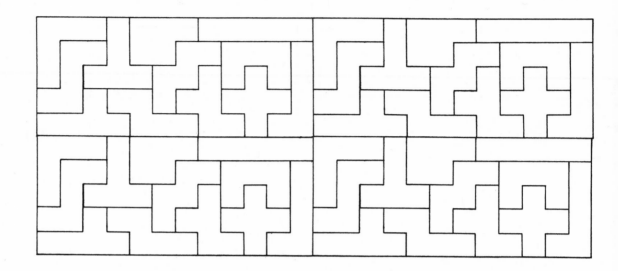

Here's an interesting pentomino alphabet constructed by R. L. Judd and M. E. Zosel and published in the *Journal of Recreational Mathematics* (11:3 [1978–79]). Try to construct your own. There are many different ways to go about making -omino alphabets.

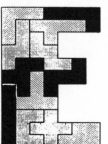 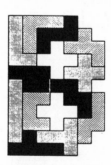 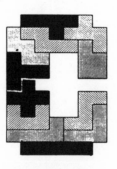 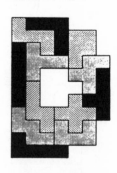

 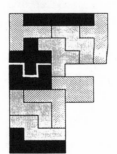 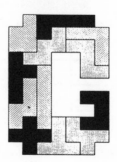 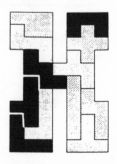

Polyominoes

As one considers orders of polyominoes greater than five (the pento-mino) and looks at the set of hexominoes or septominoes, the situation becomes increasingly complex. There are 35 possible hexominoes and 108 septominoes, as the following illustration shows:

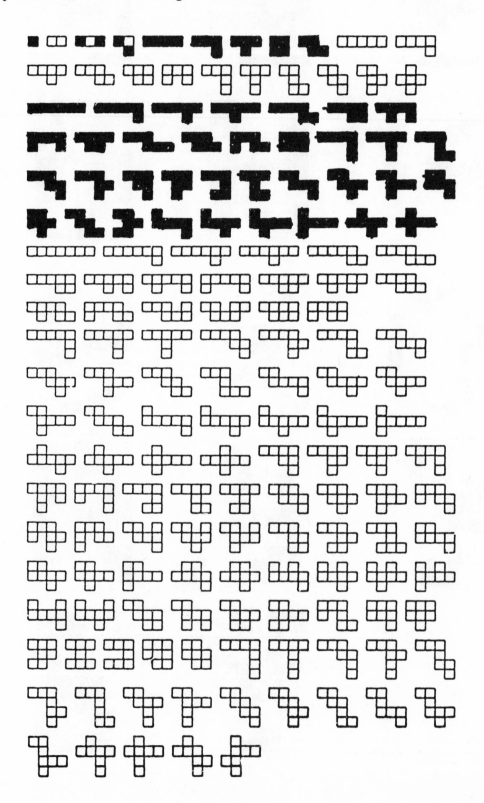

Here is a list of the number of distinct polyominoes from 1 to 18. (If you have a year or two to spare, you might want to construct a set of 19-ominoes).

1. 1
2. 1
3. 2
4. 5
5. 12
6. 35
7. 108
8. 369
9. 1,285
10. 4,655
11. 17,073
12. 63,600
13. 238,591
14. 901,971
15. 3,426,576
16. 13,079,255
17. 50,107,911
18. 192,622,052

As a final note, there is still no simple mathematical formula, given any integer n, that will calculate the number of n-ominoes.

The Planiverse

Tessellations provide adventures in the two-dimensional plane. In order to get a feel for planar life and the adventures one can have exploring plane geometry, this is a good place to take a trip to a world on the plane—the "Planiverse" created by A. K. Dewdney and some of his students at the University of Western Ontario in London, Canada.

The following book, of which I am not so much the author as compiler, originates with the being whose picture appears on the title page. His name is Yendred and he inhabits a two-dimensional space I call "the Planiverse." The discovery of the Planiverse, a reality still not accepted by many people, makes an interesting story in itself, and the purpose of this introduction is to tell it.

The first contact with Yendred was made on one of our computer terminals only a year ago. We, my students and I, had been running a program called 2DWORLD, the result of several consecutive class projects carried from one term to the next. Originally designed to give students experience in scientific stimulation and in large-scale programming projects, 2DWORLD soon took on a life of its own.

Thus begins one of the most delightful and mathematically and scientifically fascinating books since *Alice's Adventures in Wonderland*. In *The Planiverse: Computer Contact with a Two-Dimensional World* (New York: Poseidon Press, 1984), A. K. Dewdney, who writes the "Computer Recreations" column for *Scientific American,* has created a believable, moving, and interesting two-dimensional world. According to Dewdney, one day one of his graduate students noticed that the computer program 2DWORLD started using words that were not part of its programmed vocabulary. After a while Dewdney and his students realized they had made contact with a student who lived on the planet Arde, a disk-shaped planet that exists in a two-dimensional plane (it's interesting that this student's name, Yendred, is suspiciously like Yendwed, which is Dewdney spelled backward). Over the course of a summer, they communicated and became involved in the science, culture, and everyday life of Arde. They followed Yendred on his pilgrimage over the planet until he broke contact with them. Yendred's last conversation with the three-dimensional Earth dwellers was:

Yendred: We cannot talk again. To talk again is of no benefit.
Dewdney: But we have so much more to learn from you.
Yendred: You cannot learn from me. Nor I from you. You do not have the knowledge.
Dewdney: What knowledge?
Yendred: The knowledge beyond thought of the reality beyond reality.
Dewdney: Would it help if we learned your philosophy and religion?
Yendred: It has not to do with what you call philosophy or religion. If you follow only thought, you will never discover the surprise which lies beyond thought.
Dewdney: What surprise?
Yendred: Unknown: "What surprise."

The computer delivered an error message and went back to the 2DWORLD program. The adventure was over. However, in *Planiverse* Dewdney shares what was learned of the nature of Arde and the Ardeans. The book takes life on a plane seriously, just as mathematicians think about eleven-dimensional spaces they have never experienced and physicists imagine themselves into black holes and antimatter. With the help of many engineers, mathematicians, scientists, and just plain recreationists,

Arde has come to take on a specific character. Some people have thought about the details of hinges on Ardean doors, others about Ardean transportation. Athletics in Arde has been considered, as well as biology, geology, sculpture, printing, weather, and so on. The book is full of diagrams that give you an idea of how things could actually work in a two-dimensional universe. Once one gets involved in Ardean thinking, play and invention take over. Anyone can explore a part of Ardean life and make a contribution to what is a growing cult of the students of Arde. I myself have discovered an Ardean antique store and junkyard, and am trying to figure out what the objects were used for. If you become hooked, Dewdney can be contacted through *Scientific American*.

Before taking a closer look at Arde, it would be useful to think a bit about life on a plane. Imagine yourself living on the surface of a piece of paper of no thickness. Your earth would be a disk whose gravity held you on its perimeter. It is the lack of thickness that you have to constantly return to in order to understand the ingenuity of the Ardeans, just as it is the inability to jump through time at will that contributes to an understanding of Earthbound life. Think for example of the simple problem of turning around on a plane surface. Suppose you looked like this:

Now, if you were in a three-dimensional world, you could simply move out of the plane, turn forward, and then make another half-turn and be faced in the opposite direction:

However, in a plane you have no thickness. You cannot get off the surface. At best, you could tumble like this:

You end up standing on your head instead of turning around. If your body and head faced in one direction, you would have to stay facing that way all your life. It might even be that in your two-dimensional world there are left- and right-facing people:

If you were left-faced and lived on the surface of a planet like Arde, which is shaped like a disk, and you wanted to have a face-to-face conversation with a right-faced friend, you'd have to circle the disk:

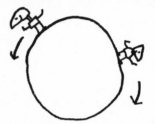

Think about what you might have to do on our globe if you wanted to pass someone. The Ardeans have solved the passing problem by allowing people to walk over each other. Of course, the problem of who walks over whom has led to many cultural conventions and not a little conflict:

Now that you've seen your first Ardeans, let's take a closer look at one of them. Remember, Ardeans have no thickness and therefore can't have skin, blood vessels, muscles, or bones, all of which function in three-dimensional space.

The first thing to notice is that Ardeans are what we would call transparent. We, in three dimensions, can see all of them. But if you were an Ardean, what would you consider your insides? They would be any parts of you blocked from your vision in the plane.

Another thing to notice is that Ardeans are built so they do not have

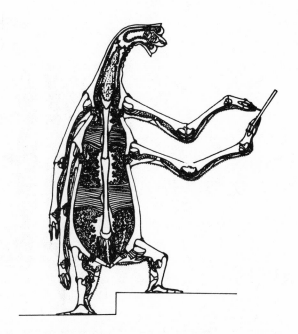

to turn around. Their bodies are symmetrical, and their heads swivel on the plane so they can face either left or right. They have four armlike structures and two feetlike structures, and are bidirectional. In a way, they are like freight trains on a single-track railroad with a locomotive at either end. Their biological structure is appropriate for life on a plane, since they cannot turn around the way we three-dimensional creatures can. Think about what would have to happen for an Ardean to turn around. He or she would have to flip over, which would mean stepping outside of the plane into three-dimensional space, as the illustration below shows. It would be like a three-dimensional creature trying to transform itself into its mirror image. There is no way that can be done in three-dimensional space.

There is one other very interesting biological adaptation to life on the plane that I want to mention. We eat and excrete. Fluids and solids pass through us. We have various tubes that exchange oxygen, that allow blood to flow, etcetera. If there were a passage through an Ardean, it would split him apart, as the picture on the next page shows.

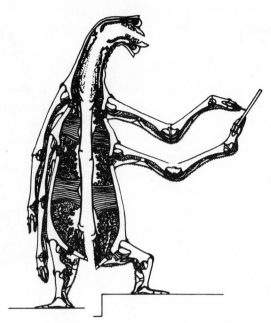

The biological adaptation of the Ardeans consisted in developing zipper organs. Here is Dewdney's account of these zipper organs:

Zipper organs are found not only in the Ardeans themselves but in virtually all lower forms, including a few plants. They occur in both muscle and nerve tissue and consist of two narrow bands of interlocking (microscopic) teeth, each flanked by a band of short, parallel chamber cells.

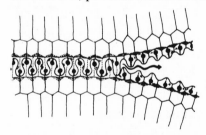

Each chamber cell is able to concentrate fluid at either end, producing, in concert with others, a bend in its section of the zipper organ. Waves of chemical excitation which pass along the organ are able to initiate a zippering or unzippering action in an unbelievably short time. In this way, fluids may be pumped through a sheet of muscle as a succession of pockets which move along its zipper.

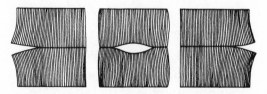

It is even possible for nerves, either isolated or embedded in muscle, to be parted and rejoined precisely without interfering in the zippering process. Naturally, this leads to a degree of intermittent neural action, but all events within the Ardean anatomy appear to be carefully timed, not unlike traffic in a large city.

I will introduce you to just a few more aspects of the Ardean world. They represent only a very small percentage of the material in the book. First, here's an Ardean house. Can you figure out why they decided to build underground? Try to analyze the ingenious method of using pulleys and moveable stairways the Ardeans have created to allow people to pass over the houses as well as enter them. Also notice the system of ramps which are used to pass from level to level.

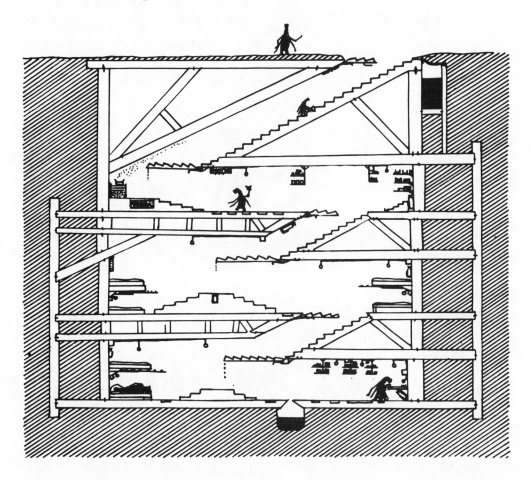

This is the conversation Dewdney and his students had with Yendred when they first were shown his home.

Dewdney: We see a house underground near you.
Yendred: That the entrance to my house is. I you inside will take.
Dewdney: We can see inside already.
Yendred: Then you like spirits are. Your eyes see through all things.
Dewdney: No. We see you from outside your space. A different dimension.

Yendred: I cannot that imagine. Is it a space beyond space?

Finally, here are pictures of an Ardean boat, which is well adapted to its planar existence, and an Ardean ball game. Traffic jams in Arde must be inevitable. You have to wait for the game to end in order to pass, or else climb over everybody. Can you figure out any ways for the Ardeans to build bypasses to alleviate their traffic problems?

Plani-diversions

Here are some exercises in planar science, mathematics, and culture for you to explore:

Draw a simple game of catch. What would a glove look like? What kind of ball would it make sense to play?
Try to transpose baseball into a Planidiversion.
Other Planidiversions:
  A counting device
  Lego blocks for children
  Dolls and how to caress them.
  Design a plani-playground and an adventure plani-playground.
  Figure out how to make sandwiches and package soft drinks.

Create a pool- and billiards-like game and a pinball machine.

Make a loom, or at least a device that would allow for something like fabric to remain together.

Explore the whole issue of glue, staples, studs, bolts, and screws—i.e., ways of holding the constructed Planiverse together.

Design musical instruments—a drum kit for example.

What would a wood stove look like? (It can't have a simple door to load the box and a flue or it would fall apart.)

Cutting Up

Another interesting exploration of the plane consists of finding ways to cut up given geometric shapes into other shapes and to construct larger shapes out of smaller ones. Here's a simple example of cutting up:

Using one cut, turn this rectangle into a square by reassembling the parts:

1 unit

4 units

(*Hint:* You can only do this if the ratio of the height to the length is 1:4.)

Here is the dissection:

2 units

1 unit

4 units

And here they are reassembled into a square:

1 unit

1 unit

2 units

Could you do the same dissection with the following rectangles? Why?

As an example of building up, copy these pieces and make a capital T out of them:

Solution:

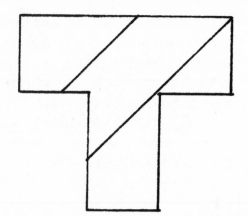

Now for a more complicated construction problem:

Copy and cut out these pieces, and make the following forms out of them. All the pieces have to be used for each construction.

Solutions:

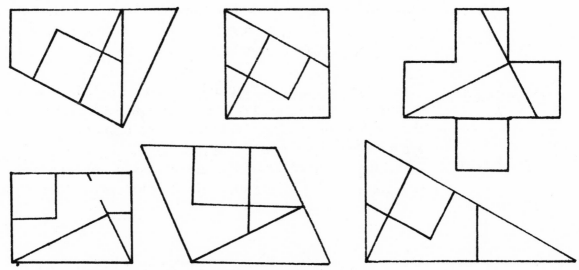

Here are a few dissection challenges:

Can you divide this big square so that it is filled by four equal-sized smaller squares?

Solution:

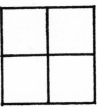

Here's a way to fit seven squares of two different sizes inside a larger square:

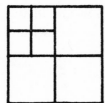

Can you completely fill a square with three smaller squares? Here are some efforts:

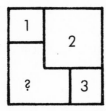 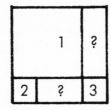 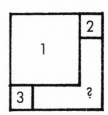

Some dissections are impossible to do. This is one. Can you figure out why?

The following dissection challenges were invented by the great English puzzler Henry Ernest Dudeney during the last part of the nineteenth century and the early twentieth. They are taken from *Henry Ernest Dudeney,* edited by Martin Gardner.

Dissecting the Letter E

Can you cut this letter E into only five pieces so that they will fit together to form a perfect square? All the measurements are given in inches so that there should be no doubt as to the correct proportions of the letter. You are not allowed to turn over any piece.

After you have solved the problem, see if you can reduce the number of pieces to four, with the added freedom to turn over any of the pieces.

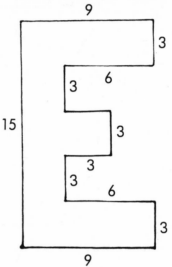

Solution:

This illustration shows how to cut the letter into five pieces that will fit together to form a perfect square, without turning over any pieces.

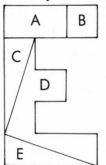 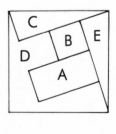

If pieces may be turned over, the dissection can be accomplished with four pieces:

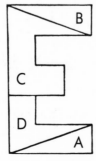 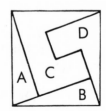

The Mutilated Cross

Here is a Greek cross (a cross as wide as it is tall) from which has been cut a square piece exactly equal to one of the arms of the cross. The puzzle is to cut what remains into four congruent* pieces that will fit together and form a square.

Solution:

The illustration shows how to cut the mutilated cross. Just continue each side of the square until you strike a corner, and there you are!

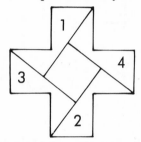 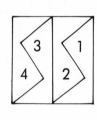

Greek Cross Puzzle

Here is a puzzle for younger people. Cut a square into four pieces in the manner shown, then put these four pieces together so as to form a Greek cross.

Solution:

Place the four pieces together in the manner shown, and the Greek cross will be found in the center.

*Congruent pieces have the same size and shape.

Square and Cross

Cut a Greek cross into five pieces, so that one piece is an entire smaller Greek cross, and so that the remaining four pieces will fit together and form a perfect square.

Solution:

If we cut the smaller Greek cross in the manner shown on the left, the four pieces A, B, C, and D will fit together and form a perfect square:

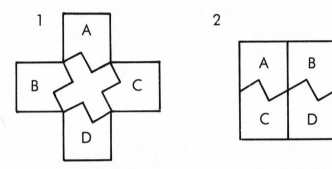

The Improvised Checkerboard

Some Englishmen at the front during World War I wished to pass a restful hour at a game of checkers. They had coins and small stones for the chess pieces, but no board. However, one of them found a piece of linoleum as shown in the illustration, and, as it contained the right number of squares, it was decided to cut it and fit the pieces together to form a board, blacking some of the squares afterward for convenience in playing.

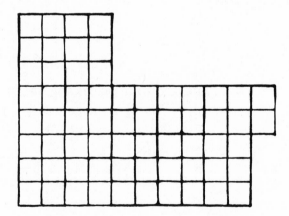

An ingenious Scotsman showed how this could be done by cutting the stuff in two pieces only, and it is a really good puzzle to discover how he did it. Cut the linoleum along the lines into two pieces that will fit together and form an 8-by-8 board.

Solution:

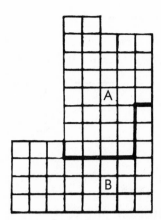

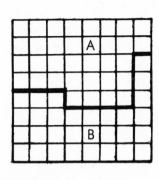

Square of Squares

Cutting only along the lines, what is the smallest number of square pieces into which the following diagram can be dissected? The largest number possible is, of course, 169, where all the pieces will be of the same size— one cell—but we want the smallest number. We might cut away the border on two sides, leaving one square 12 by 12, and cutting the remainder in 25 little squares, making 26 in all. This is better than 169, but considerably more than the fewest possible.

Solution:

There is, we believe, only one solution to this puzzle, shown here. The fewest pieces must be 11, the portions must be of the sizes given, the 3 largest pieces must be arranged as shown, and the remaining group of 8 squares may be reflected but cannot be arranged differently with respect to each other.

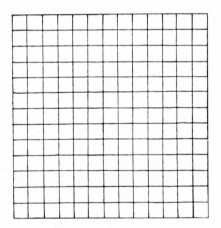

You can make your own dissections and use them as puzzles for your friends to solve. For example, start with a given shape and then play around with dissecting it. You might begin with a triangle and cut it up in different ways:

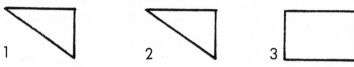

Then cut out the parts (be sure to keep a copy of the original dissection) and you have the following puzzle:

Ask your friends to make one large right triangle using these three shapes.

Symmetry

So far, this discussion of patterns has been exploring aspects of the whole plane. We will now focus briefly on internal aspects of some two-dimensional shapes. The first part will deal with symmetry. We will then go on to look at the systematic modification of regular shapes such as squares and triangles, which gives rise to forms called fractals.

Mathematics and art often converge. Several years ago I came upon an introduction to the concept of symmetry written by Claudia Zaslavsky. She uses fabric designs created by the Asante people of Ghana to illustrate the concepts of axial and rotational symmetry. Here is an edited version.

The Asante people of Ghana wear adinkra cloth on special occasions. The word *adinkra* means "saying goodbye," and originally this cloth was worn only in times of mourning. Designs are printed on the cloth by means of stamps cut on pieces of calabash and dipped in black dye. Usually these stamps have symbolic meaning. The heart-shaped stamp, 1, means "take heart," or have patience. Design 2 symbolizes "unity is strength."

Line, or Axial, Symmetry

Compare the left and right halves of these two adinkra stamps.

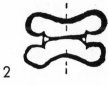

If you place a mirror or a rectangle of colored transparent plastic upright on the dotted line, you will see that the reflection exactly matches the section hidden by the mirror.

If you fold a sheet of paper once, paint the left-hand part of the design to the left of the fold, and then press the folded paper while the paint is wet, you can reproduce the design.

If you cut a stencil having only half the design, you can trace the whole pattern by flipping your stencil over.

The dotted line in figure 2 is called an *axis* (or *line*) *of symmetry*.

Is there an axis of symmetry in adinkra stamp 3?

Look at stamp 2 again. Can you find another axis of symmetry? The stamp has two perpendicular lines of symmetry.

Rotational Symmetry

Now look at adinkra stamp 3 again. Rotate the page a half-turn, through an angle of 180 degrees (that is, turn it upside down). The design appears the same.

3

Place a large dot in the center of the pattern. If you carved half the design on a stamp (a linoleum block, for example), you could reproduce the whole pattern. You would use your stamp twice, keeping one point of the stamp fixed on the center, and rotating it to produce the other half. Can you carve less than half of this pattern on the stamp, and still reproduce the whole design?

Design 3 has *rotational symmetry*. The *basic region* of the design is the smallest part that you can carve on a stamp in order to reproduce the design. Stamp 3 has rotational symmetry of *order two*, because there are two different positions in which the figure appears the same.

Let us analyze the gold weight, figure 4. For several centuries, Asante merchants supplied most of the gold used in the currencies of Europe. They balanced the gold dust against these weights, beautiful brass objects crafted in thousands of different patterns.

4

Figure 4 has ten axes of symmetry. This is the basic region that you would cut into a stencil.

You need to use the stencil twenty times, flipping it over, to reproduce the complete design.

Figure 4 has rotational symmetry of *order ten*. Here is one basic region that you could carve on a stamp, but it is not the only one.

You would use the stamp ten times, rotating it 36 degrees each time (360 ÷ 10).

In the pictures below, analyze each figure for line symmetry. Sketch *the* basic region.

Then analyze each figure for rotational symmetry. Sketch *a* basic region.

Talons of   Ram's Horns   Unity   Adinkra
the Eagle   (Concealment)   King

Four Asante Adinkra Stamps (Ghana)

 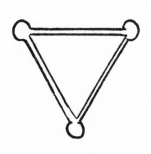 

Gold Weight   Gold Weight   Brass Lid to
Gold-Dust Box

The Gold-Dust Trade (Asante, Ghana)

Here is another exercise in symmetry:

Write down the alphabet (both upper- and lower-case letters) and the digits from 0 to 9:

ABCDEFGHIJKLMNOPQRSTUVWXYZ
abcdefghijklmnopqrstuvwxyz
0123456789

Now examine each letter and see if it has axial or rotational symmetry. If you find an axis of symmetry, draw it through the letter.

How many letters and numbers have a vertical axis of symmetry? A horizontal axis? A diagonal one? How many have rotational symmetry? How many are not symmetrical?

A   B   C   D   E   F   G   H   I   J   K   L   M

N   O   P   Q   R   S   T   U   V   W   X   Y   Z

Horizontal	Vertical	Rotational	None
9	11	7	7

Which aspects of the human body are symmetrical and which aren't? How many axes of symmetry does a circle have?

Following are a number of suggestions about playing with symmetry drawn from the Nuffield Mathematics Teaching Project unit on symmetry. The following three patterns have been drawn using a ruler and a compass. If you hold each one to a mirror, it will look the same as its reflection. Two of them will look the same if you hold the page upside down.

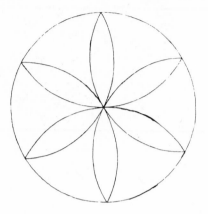 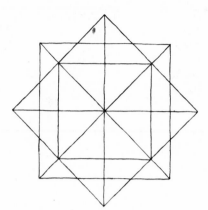 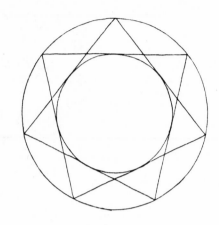

Using a ruler and a compass, draw two patterns of your own, each of which looks the same when held up to a mirror or when held upside down. You may make the patterns as complicated as you like.

The small shape is like the tee a golfer uses to place his ball on. Use this shape to make up a pattern that looks the same when it is held up to a mirror or when it is held upside down.

Take a sheet of paper or newspaper and fold it in two. Cut out a piece as shown on the left, below. You may make the piece any shape you like. How many holes will appear in the paper when you unfold it?

Fold another piece of paper, this time making a *second* fold at right angles to the first, as shown on the right. Cut out a piece working from the line of the second fold. How many separate pieces have you cut out?

Repeat the last process, but fold the paper *three* times at right angles before making a cut, working from the last fold.

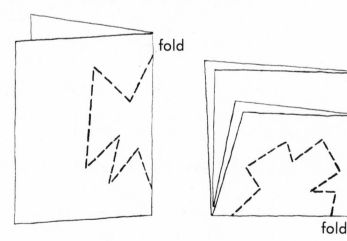

Now fold a piece of paper, along *parallel* lines before you cut out a shape from the final fold position, as shown below left.

Another way is to fold a sheet of paper twice at right angles and then fold it *obliquely,* as below right, before cutting out a shape from the last fold line.

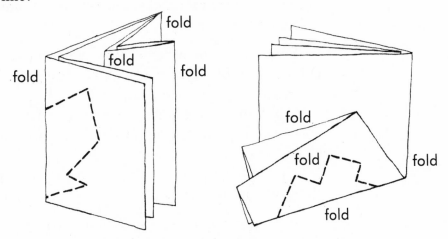

Each time, count the number of folds you make and the number of pieces you have cut out. Write these facts down.

Try folding and cutting circular discs of paper in different ways. These often give decorative patterns too.

If you get an interesting pattern of holes, copy it using better paper. Make a collection of three or four really different patterns that were made by folding several paper shapes in a variety of ways.

Fold a piece of plain paper in two and mark the fold well by pressing your thumb along it. Pierce a small hole through the folded paper, using a pin or the point of a compass. Open the paper out. You will see two holes in it.

How are the holes related
    to each other?
    to the mark of the fold on the paper?
(*Hint:* Join the holes with a pencil line.)

If you pierce other holes in the folded paper, will they be related in the same way?

Fold a piece of paper in two, and then in two again, making the folds *parallel.* Pierce a small hole through the folded paper and open the paper out. How many holes are there in the paper?

How are the holes related
    to one another?
    to the folds in the paper?

(*Hint:* It may help you to number the holes and to mark the lines of the folds with letters of the alphabet.)

Fold a piece of paper several times, making the folds *parallel.* Pierce a hole through the folded paper and open the paper out. Are the holes related to one another and to the folds in the same way as they were in the previous two exercises?

Fold a piece of paper in two and then make a second fold at right angles to the first. Pierce a small hole through the folded paper. Before you unfold the paper, write down:

how many holes you expect to see when you unfold it

the shape of the figure you will make if you join the holes, in a clockwise direction, with pencil lines.

Unfold the paper and check that you were right. How are the holes related to one another and to the folds in the paper?

If the pencil lines joining the holes you made form a square, can you say why? If they do not form a square, can you suggest where the hole must be pierced if you want the lines to form a square?

Fold the paper *three* times, making each fold at right angles to the previous fold. Pierce a hole through the folded paper and write down:

the number of holes you expect to see when you open the paper

how you think they will be related to one another and to the folds in the paper.

Repeat the last exercise with *four* folds in the paper.

Together, these exercises show that:

holes made in folded paper will lie on a number of straight lines

holes will be equidistant from certain axes of symmetry

the lines joining holes made in this way will be at right angles to certain axes of symmetry

making more folds produces more holes, for a particular piercing position

the *number* of holes made, for a certain number of right-angle, oblique, or parallel folds, is the same for a similar piercing position

it is the *arrangement* of holes that differs according to the folding style, sequence of folds, and piercing position.

Folds, Holes, and Axes

If *one* fold, AB, is made, the relationship between the holes and the fold is a simple one:

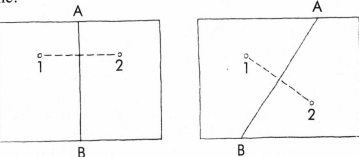

If *several parallel* folds are made, the holes will be symmetrically placed about more than one axis—here, AB, CD and EF.

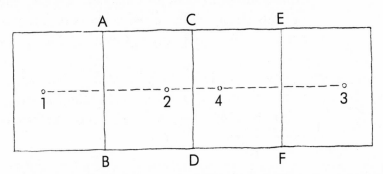

If *two* folds, AB and CD, are made in the paper at *right angles,* the four holes will lie at the vertices of a rectangle, though they may possibly lie at the vertices of that particular rectangle we call a square.

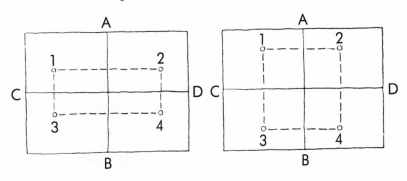

In the five diagrams, the numbered holes are symmetrically placed about axes as follows:

Axes	First Pair	Long Diagram	Last Pair
AB	1 and 2	1 and 2	1 and 2
CD	—	1 and 3; 2 and 4	1 and 3; 2 and 4
EF	—	3 and 4	—

The particular case of a square pattern of holes is considered further below.

Reflection of Point in Axes

One axis: Two holes may be taken to represent a point and its image by reflection in an axis of symmetry. The distance of the point from the axis of symmetry will be the same as the distance of its image from the axis of symmetry.

More than one axis: For a point reflected in more than one axis of symmetry, the distance between the point and its images need not be equal. In particular, the distances between a point and its two images obtained by placing the point randomly near the junction of two mirrors set at right angles to each other are *unlikely* to be equal. If they are not equal, the point and its images (including the double image by reflection in both axes) will lie at the vertices of a rectangle. It is when the distances are *equal* that the point and its images lie at the vertices of a square.

Fold Sequence and Piercing Position for a Square Pattern of Holes

For holes to lie at the vertices of a square, fold the paper twice with the folds at right angles. Then bring the folds together to make a third fold at an angle of 45 degrees with each of the other two. Lastly, pierce the hole somewhere *along* this third fold.

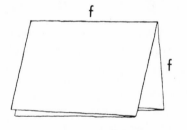 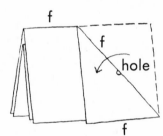

Making Hole Patterns

Many different patterns of holes can result by varying the folding sequence and piercing position. You may enjoy trying those in the table below, but you will learn most by devising your own. All layers of paper need to be pierced when making a hole.

Pattern	Folding	No. of holes	Piercing Position
Square	2 at right angles 1 at 45° to other two	4	along third fold
Rectangle	3 at right angles	8	a general one
2 Nested Rectangles	4 at right angles	16 (12 + 4)	a general one
Octagon	2 at right angles 1 at 45° to other two	8	a general one
Regular Octagon	2 at right angles 1 at 45° to other two	8	on bisector of angle between folds

The angle bisector for the last item can be found by making a fourth fold, shown dotted below. (It is a particular oblique fold.)

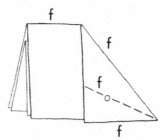

In the section on tessellations, we saw that there were only three regular polygons—the equilateral triangle, the square, and the hexagon—that tessellate the plane. How many axes of symmetry do each of these shapes have?

With a knowledge of symmetry, you can now create more complex tilings and tessellations. Here are some construction techniques provided by Peter S. Stevens in his *Handbook of Regular Patterns*. Notice that different properties of symmetry are used to create repeating and merging patterns.

Figure 1 shows a Moorish design in the Alhambra in Spain. After M. C. Escher visited the Alhambra and carefully copied the design in figure 2, he produced the pattern of beetles in figure 3.

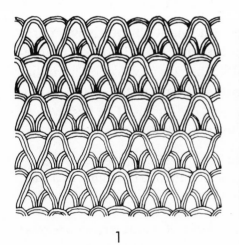

1

2

3

Creating the Fundamental Region

The essential ingredients of this fundamental region (see next page) are two twofold rotations and a reflection. Consequently, to make patterns of fundamental regions, simply draw a row of alternating twofold centers between two mirror lines as illustrated in figure 4a. Then draw identical lines with twofold rotation through one set of centers, as shown in frame 4b, and a different set of identical lines with twofold rotation through the other set, as in frame 4c. Reflecting these lines in the mirrors produces the outline of heads in frame 4d.

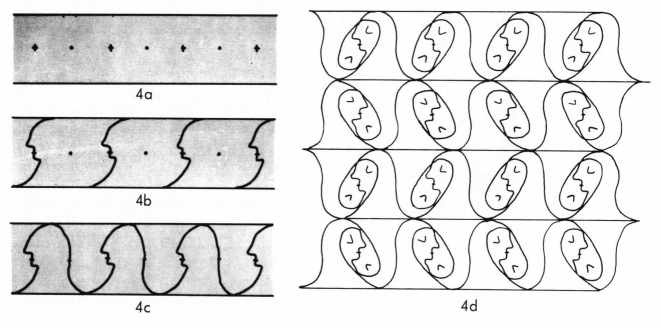

4a

4b

4c

4d

Fractals

The Fractal Geometry of Nature, by Benoit Mandelbrot (New York: W. H. Freeman, 1982), is as beautiful and interesting a book on mathematics as any I've ever seen. Mandelbrot's work on developing a mathematical language to describe irregular forms such as coastlines and mountain peaks led him to develop the growing field of fractals. The best way to introduce fractals is by listening to Mandelbrot himself:

> Why is geometry often described as "cold" and "dry"? One reason lies in its inability to describe the shape of a cloud, a mountain, a coastline, or a tree. Clouds are not spheres, mountains are not cones, coastlines are not circles, and bark is not smooth, nor does lightning travel in a straight line.
>
> More generally, I claim that many patterns of nature are so irregular and fragmented, that, compared with *Euclid*—a term used in this work to denote all of standard geometry—nature exhibits not simply a higher degree but an altogether different level of complexity. The number of distinct scales of length of natural patterns is for all practical purposes infinite.
>
> The existence of these patterns challenges us to study those forms that Euclid leaves aside as being "formless," to investigate the morphology of the "amorphous." Mathematicians have disdained this challenge, however, and have increasingly chosen to flee from nature by devising theories unrelated to anything we can see or feel.

Responding to this challenge, I conceived and developed a new geometry of nature and implemented its use in a number of diverse fields. It describes many of the irregular and fragmented patterns around us, and leads to full-fledged theories, by identifying a family of shapes I call *fractals*. The most useful fractals involve *chance,* and both their regularities and their irregularities are statistical. Also, the shapes described here tend to be *scaling,* implying that the degree of their irregularity and/or fragmentation is identical at all scales. The concept of *fractal* (Hausdorff) *dimension* plays a central role in this work.

Some fractal sets are curves or surfaces, others are disconnected "dusts," and yet others are so oddly shaped that there are no good terms for them in either the sciences or the arts. . . .

I coined *fractal* from the Latin adjective *fractus.* The corresponding Latin verb *frangere* means "to break": to create irregular fragments. It is therefore sensible—and how appropriate for our needs!—that, in addition to "fragmented" (as in *fraction* or *refraction*), *fractus* should also mean "irregular," both meanings being preserved in *fragment.*

The proper pronunciation is *frac'tal,* the stress being placed as in *frac'tion.*

Here are two examples of fractals:

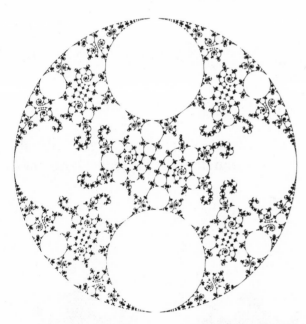

SELF-HOMOGRAPHIC FRACTAL

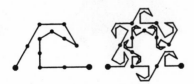

MONKEYS TREE

Let's take a look at how fractals evolve. One starts with a simple form, say a right angle with two sides of equal length. Then apply a modification like this one to each side:

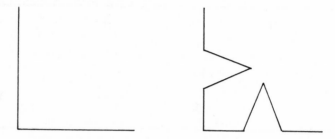

At the next step, continue the modification, only do it to every segment of the already modified form:

Then do it again:

The resulting curve, which is becoming longer and longer in small steps, begins to assume a shape that has something of the feel of coastlines one sees outlined on maps.

Here is one of Mandelbrot's illustrations of the first few steps in the development of a fractal curve.

Patterns on the Plane

Below are the patterns of development of some fractals.

Notice that figure 2 is a Rep-Tile (see p. 27).

Here are the first two steps in the development of some fractal curves. Try to imagine what the curves will look like after two more steps. Then draw them. You'll probably need a large sheet of paper and a very sharp pencil.

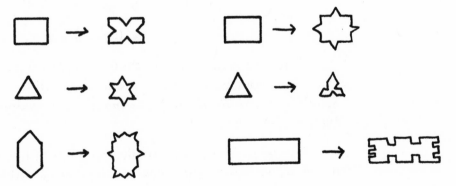

Getting It Straight

Finally, one more bit of play on the plane. This has to do with drawing straight lines through an array of points. Here's a problem to start with:

Draw a line consisting of no more than four segments through all nine dots. The line should start at one dot and end at a different one. The segments can intersect each other.

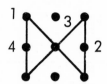

Here was my first effort:

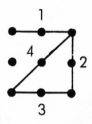

And my next:

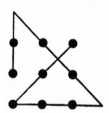

After a while I gave up on this puzzle and asked the friend who showed it to me what the answer was. This is the drawing she produced. It had never occurred to me that the lines could extend beyond the points. The solution required a more open conception of the problem than mine.

Here are some similar, though more difficult, challenges. Try the challenges yourself before you read the analysis, which comes from Fred Schuh's *Master Book of Mathematical Recreations* (New York: Dover, 1968).

Problem: What is the smallest number of line segments that will join these twelve dots? The lines can cross each other but must make one continuous path and join up at the end.

The smallest number of line segments to produce a continuous line that satisfies the requirements is five:

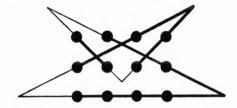

By deleting one of the three lightly drawn sections of the closed broken line, we get an open broken line that satisfies the condition.

Apart from these three solutions, which begin at a dot and end at a dot, we have the sixteen solutions shown below, which cannot be completed to form a closed broken line without increasing the number of line segments.

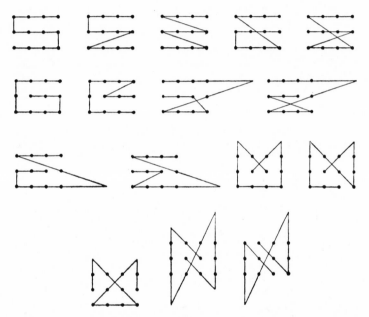

It is easy enough to find a broken line of five segments that runs through the twelve dots, because some of the solutions are very obvious. The difficulty consists entirely in finding the whole set of solutions.

Number Patterns

Each problem that I solved became a rule that served afterward to solve other problems.
—Descartes, *Discourse on Method*

Playing with Numbers

I have always loved to play with numbers. When I was in elementary school, I remember making a number–letter equivalence chart with 1 = A, 2 = B, 3 = C, etc., and getting a sum as the numeric representation of the names of all the people in my class. Thus, I was Herbert: 8 + 5 + 18 + 2 + 5 + 18 +20 = 76. My friend Ronald was 18 + 15 + 14 + 1 + 12 + 4 = 64. I didn't stop there, but either grouped students with the same numeric equivalents for their names or took the digits representing a name (76 and 64 for me and Ronnie) and then played with those digits. Thus, the digits of 76 (7 + 6) could produce the sum 13, which was a prime number.* Then the digits of 13 would lead to 1 + 3 = 4. Ronnie's 64 leads to 6 + 4 = 10, and the digits of 10 add up to 1. Thus my key numbers were 76, 13, and 4; Ronnie's were 64, 10, and 1.

So what?

That's what many of my friends used to say, though they always wanted to know what their key numbers were. And their question was proper. I had nothing metaphysical or mystical in mind. It was just a pleasant way to pass time, more pleasant than filling out the practice sheets handed out by my teacher, which I frequently turned in incomplete. And it led to my asking further questions and building up minisystems and articulating and trying to prove theorems—though I didn't know that was what I was doing.

For example, I remember experimenting with different ways of coding the alphabet with the numbers 1 to 26, with the goal of getting minimal and maximal sums for Ronnie and me as compared to the coded names of the rest of our friends.

Numbers have always seemed interesting to me, and I was delighted a few years ago when a friend mentioned he had discovered a proof that there was no uninteresting integer. The proof was attributed to the Indian mathematical genius Srinivasa Ramanujan who, as a boy, taught himself number theory, re-proved most of the main theorems in the field, and invented new ones without any formal mathematical training. According to my friend, Ramanujan once heard a mathematician call a certain integer uninteresting and replied that he had a proof that no integer was uninteresting. The proof is quite easy to follow:

Suppose there are uninteresting integers. Then there must be a list of

---

*A prime number is a number that cannot be divided by any other positive number (except itself and 1) without resulting in a fraction.

uninteresting integers and a smallest number on the list. Call it x.

However, x has the interesting characteristic of being the smallest uninteresting integer. Therefore, x cannot be the smallest uninteresting integer.

At this point the second number on the list becomes the smallest uninteresting integer. But the same argument applies to it and all the other numbers on the list.

Therefore, there is no uninteresting integer.

Ramanujan's argument got me to thinking about the unexpected characteristics of seemingly uninteresting numbers. For example, on the surface, 17 seems like a good candidate for uninteresting number of the year. It's a prime number, and its digits add up to 8, which is an interesting number. Nothing much else seems to stand out about it.

One afternoon while I was waiting to be served lunch at a crowded and slow restaurant, I started fooling around with 17. One of the pleasures of playing with mathematics is that you don't need anything more elaborate than pencil and paper, and a little time. Well, I began by doubling 17, and then adding the digits of the answer together:

$$2 \times 17 = 34 \text{ and } 3 + 4 = 7$$

I knew that the sum of the digits of 1×17 was 8. Perhaps there was a pattern, and the sum of the digits of 3×17 would be 6. Sure enough:

$$3 \times 17 = 51 \text{ and } 5 + 1 = 6$$

Now the game became intriguing.

$$4 \times 17 = 68, \text{ and } 6 + 8 = 14, \text{ and, adding again, } 4 + 1 = 5$$

Could I get all the way to 1 by subsequent multiplication of 17? Here are the results:

$$5 \times 17 = 85 \qquad 8 + 5 = 13 \text{ and } 1 + 3 = 4$$
$$6 \times 17 = 102 \qquad 1 + 0 + 2 = 3$$
$$7 \times 17 = 119 \qquad 1 + 1 + 9 = 11 \text{ and } 1 + 1 = 2$$
$$8 \times 17 = 136 \qquad 1 + 3 + 6 = 10 \text{ and } 1 + 0 = 1$$

I got a consistent run from 8 down to 1, a very curious fact about the previously uninteresting 17.

I wished I had a calculator with me so I could see where the sequence went after it got down to 1. It might repeat itself, or scatter and become random. When I got home, I calculated out to 17×15. Here are the results:

$17 \times$	Sum of Digits
9	9
10	8
11	7
12	6
13	5
14	4
15	3

I had to go on for at least three more multiples.

$17 \times$	Sum of Digits
16	2
17	1
18	9

I found myself getting very excited. Had anyone ever noticed my discovery about 17 before? Would it hold for any sequence of multiples no matter how large? Was the pattern a repeating pattern which would represent some repeating decimal and therefore a fraction? Could I develop a proof or explanation of the pattern? I decided to carry around my pocket calculator and continue my exploration of 17 as well as of the repeating pattern:

$$987654321987654321987654321 \ldots$$

These explorations are still in progress.

It might be fun for you to try something similar. Pick a number that initially seems uninteresting, and (with the help of a calculator if you happen to have one) explore its multiples, the sum of its digits, the way it responds to different additions and subtractions. Here are a few numbers that come to mind:

31   43   57   61   71

The number 71 interests me because it is the reverse of 17. Does it have similar repeating properties? Well, $7 + 1 = 8$ and

$$71 \times 2 = 142 \qquad 1 + 4 + 2 = 7$$
$$71 \times 3 = 213 \qquad \text{which gives } 6$$
$$71 \times 4 = 284 \qquad \text{which gives } 5$$
$$71 \times 5 = 355 \qquad \text{which gives } 4$$

Here we go again. I did not expect this partial result when I picked 71. As is quite usual in mathematics, explorations lead to other explorations as soon as the habit of playing is developed.

Recently 71 popped into my life again. I was skimming through an issue of the *Journal of Recreational Mathematics,* where I discovered some mystical properties classically ascribed to 71:

a) Ancient transhimalayan occultists claim in their books that creation began with 1,065 rays of light. But 1,065 = 71 × 15.

b) According to the Cabala's number-letter code of old Judaism, both the deity of the East (Brahma) and of the West (God) are numerically equal to 71 × 2 and 71 respectively.

c) The only chapter of Numbers in the Bible which contains enough verses to require 71 headings is chapter 7, and verse 7:71 reads: "and for the sacrifice of peace offerings, *2* oxen, *5* rams, *5* goats, and *5* male lambs *one* year old." But 2,555 + one = 2,556 = 1 + 2 + 3 + 4 + . . . + 71.

The Elegant Nine

A number with what might be called an elegant personality is 9, and you might like to begin an exploration of numeric personality with the 9's table. Fill in this table and then add the sums of the digits of the answers. What do you notice?

9 ×	Sum of Digits
1	
2	
3	
4	
5	
6	
7	
8	
9	
10	

Now try bigger numbers, just as I did with multiples of 17, and keep on adding the digits of the answers until you get a single-digit answer. What do you notice about your first, second, and (if your number is large enough) subsequent additions? You may want to start with these:

9 ×	=	= Sum of Digits	= Sum of Digits
11	99	18	9
12			
13			
14			
15			
23			
25			
51			
71			
456			
654			
12,456			

Here are some more 9 explorations:

A
9×9 =
99×99 =
999×999 =
9999×9999 =
99999×99999 =

B
9×7 =
99×77 =
999×777 =
9999×7777 =
99999×77777 =

C
9×1 + 2 =
9×12 + 3 =
9×123 + 4 =
9×1234 + 5 =
9×12345 + 6 =
9×123456 + 7 =
9×1234567 + 8 =
9×12345678 + 9 =
9×123456789 + 10 =

D
9×9 + 7 =
9×98 + 6 =
9×987 + 5 =
9×9876 + 4 =
9×98765 + 3 =
9×987654 + 2 =
9×9876543 + 1 =
9×98765432 + 0 =

E
12345679×9 =
12345679×18 =
12345679×27 =
12345679×36 =
12345679×45 =
12345679×54 =
12345679×63 =
12345679×72 =
12345679×81 =

Solutions:

A
9×9 = 81
99×99 = 9801
999×999 = 998001
9999×9999 = 99980001
99999×99999 = 9999800001

B
9×7 = 63
99×77 = 7623
999×777 = 776223
9999×7777 = 77762223
99999×77777 = 7777622223

C
9×1 + 2 = 11
9×12 + 3 = 111
9×123 + 4 = 1111
9×1234 + 5 = 11111
9×12345 + 6 = 111111
9×123456 + 7 = 1111111
9×1234567 + 8 = 11111111
9×12345678 + 9 = 111111111
9×123456789 + 10 = 1111111111

The Elegant Nine

	D				E
9×9	$+ 7$	$= 88$		$12345679 \times 9 =$	111111111
9×98	$+ 6$	$= 888$		$12345679 \times 18 =$	222222222
9×987	$+ 5$	$= 8888$		$12345679 \times 27 =$	333333333
9×9876	$+ 4$	$= 88888$		$12345679 \times 36 =$	444444444
9×98765	$+ 3$	$= 888888$		$12345679 \times 45 =$	555555555
9×987654	$+ 2$	$= 8888888$		$12345679 \times 54 =$	666666666
9×9876543	$+ 1$	$= 88888888$		$12345679 \times 63 =$	777777777
9×98765432	$+ 0$	$= 888888888$		$12345679 \times 72 =$	888888888
				$12345679 \times 81 =$	999999999

Nine is a pretty amazing digit. If you tried to do any of the exercises, you'll have discovered that 9 generates some unexpected and interesting number patterns. You'll have also discovered that when you multiply 9 by any number and add the digits together, a multiple of 9 results. Continued adding always leaves you with a final 9. Similar multiplying and adding with 17 led to a sequence. Nine always returns to itself, which is why it was regarded as the symbol for indestructible matter in ancient times.

Casting Nines into the Water

This so-called indestructible character of 9 is the principle of the "casting out of nines" which depends upon the fact that any number whose digits add up to 9 or a multiple of 9 must be evenly divisible by 9. It leads to an interesting trick. Pick any number whose digits do not add up to 9; say, 445,578. The digits add up to 33, which is not a multiple of 9. You can easily check that 445,578 is not evenly divisible by 9 (the answer, rounded off to one decimal place, comes out 49,508.7). Now all you have to do is add a digit to your original number so that the sum of the new number's digits will be divisible by 9 and the resulting number will also be divisible by 9 *no matter where in that original number you add the new digit.* The digits of our number add up to 33, so all we have to do is insert the digit 3 somewhere; then the sum of the digits will be 36, which is divisible by 9. Check for yourself that all of the following numbers are divisible by 9 and then share your sophistication with some of your friends:

3,445,578   4,345,578   4,435,578
4,453,578   4,455,378   4,455,738   4,455,783

Numeric Experimentation

Experiment with the multiples of other numbers. Try 7's, 6's, or 5's. Or 11, 29—just about any number. See whether the assumption that the sum of the digits of the multiples of any number creates a predictable sequence seems to hold.

Let's consider multiples of 7 and the sum of their digits as an example:

	7	14	21	28	35	42	49	56	63	70
Sum of digits:	7	5	3	10	8	6	13	11	9	7

There may be a pattern. The numbers 7, 5, 3 are descending consecutive odd numbers; 10, 8, 6 are descending consecutive even numbers; and 13, 11, 9, 7 are descending odd numbers. Perhaps, if one kept on examining multiples of 7, a recurring pattern would emerge.

I can't resist trying another six:

	77	84	91	98	105	112
Sum of digits:	14	12	10	17	6	4

The appearance of 17 is a bit puzzling, but there may still be some regular sequence. If you have some time to spare, try to find it and let me know what you come up with. If you are sure no regular sequence will result, also let me know as irregularity is also an interesting mathematical property.

Add a sequence of numbers to the multiples of a given number (as in examples C and D on pp. 85–86) and see if interesting sequences develop.

Here's an example. Consider the sequence of every other even number:

$$2, 6, 10, 14, 18, 22, \ldots$$

and the multiples of 3:

$$3, 6, 9, 12, 15, 18, \ldots$$

Now add the sequences term by term:

2	6	10	14	18	22
+3	+6	+ 9	+12	+15	+18
5	12	19	26	33	40

And now explore the new sequence:

$$5, 12, 19, 26, 33, 40$$

Here are two more interesting multiplications to try:

$37 \times \ 3 =$	8×1	$+ \ 1 \ =$
$\times \ 6 =$	8×12	$+ \ 2 \ =$
$\times \ 9 =$	8×123	$+ \ 3 \ =$
$\times \ 12 =$	8×1234	$+ \ 4 \ =$
$\times \ 15 =$	8×12345	$+ \ 5 \ =$
$\times \ 18 =$	8×123456	$+ \ 6 \ =$
$\times \ 21 =$	8×1234567	$+ \ 7 \ =$
$\times \ 24 =$	8×12345678	$+ \ 8 \ =$
$\times \ 27 =$	8×123456789	$+ \ 9 \ =$

Solutions:

$37 \ \times 3 = 111$	8×1	$+ \ 1 \ = 9$
$\times 6 = 222$	8×12	$+ \ 2 \ = 98$
$\times 9 = 333$	8×123	$+ \ 3 \ = 987$
$\times 12 = 444$	8×1234	$+ \ 4 \ = 9876$
$\times 15 = 555$	8×12345	$+ \ 5 \ = 98765$
$\times 18 = 666$	8×123456	$+ \ 6 \ = 987654$
$\times 21 = 777$	8×1234567	$+ \ 7 \ = 9876543$
$\times 24 = 888$	8×12345678	$+ \ 8 \ = 98765432$
$\times 27 = 999$	8×123456789	$+ \ 9 \ = 987654321$

The technique of adding the digits of a given number can become a very complex activity. Here is a short article by Nobuyuki Yoshigahara (*Journal of Recreational Mathematics* 11:4 [1978–79]) in which the squares of the digits of numbers are added together, leading to interesting loops of numbers.

Take a natural number (for example 1977). Cut the number into single digits and add up their squares;

$$1977 \rightarrow 1^2 + 9^2 + 7^2 + 7^2 = 180$$

Apply this transformation to the result.

$$180 \rightarrow 1^2 + 8^2 + 0^2 = 65$$

Repeat this in turn. This process enters into an eight-membered loop as follows:

$$1977 \rightarrow 180 \rightarrow 65 \rightarrow 61 \rightarrow 37 \rightarrow 58 \rightarrow 89 \rightarrow 145$$
$$\uparrow \qquad\qquad\qquad\qquad \downarrow$$
$$16 \leftarrow 4 \leftarrow 20 \leftarrow 42$$

Another kind of destination is shown below:

$$14515 \rightarrow 68 \rightarrow 100 \rightarrow 1$$

This 1 can be considered to be a one-membered loop.

By such successive transformation, all natural numbers enter into one of the two loops shown above.

I developed this idea further. I cut the numbers into two digits at a time from the right.

$$1977 \rightarrow 19^2 + 77^2 = 6{,}290 \rightarrow 62^2 + 90^2 = 11944 \rightarrow 1^2 + 19^2 + 44^2 = 2298$$

Starting from 1977, such successive transformation gave a long side-track and a huge loop (fifty-six–membered):

$$1977 \rightarrow 6290 \rightarrow 11944 \rightarrow 2298 \rightarrow 10088 \rightarrow 7745 \rightarrow 7954 \rightarrow 9157 \rightarrow 11530 \rightarrow 1126 \rightarrow 797$$
$$\downarrow$$
$$3925 \leftarrow 962 \leftarrow 1129 \leftarrow 2027 \leftarrow 10145 \leftarrow 8849 \leftarrow 6865 \leftarrow 7241 \leftarrow 485 \leftarrow 12200 \leftarrow 9458$$
$$\downarrow$$
$$2146 \rightarrow 2557 \rightarrow 3874 \rightarrow 6920 \rightarrow 5161 \rightarrow 6322 \rightarrow 4453 \rightarrow 4745 \rightarrow 4234 \rightarrow 2920 \rightarrow 1241 \rightarrow 1825 \rightarrow 949$$
$$\downarrow$$
$$5329 \ \leftarrow \ 7300 \ \leftarrow \ 2482$$
$$\swarrow$$

$12832 \rightarrow 1809 \rightarrow 405 \rightarrow 41 \rightarrow 1681 \rightarrow 6817 \rightarrow 4913 \rightarrow 2570 \rightarrow 5525 \rightarrow 3650 \rightarrow 3796 \rightarrow 10585$		
$\uparrow$		$\downarrow$
7684		7251
$\uparrow$		$\downarrow$
5072		7785
$\uparrow$		$\downarrow$
4456		13154
$\uparrow$		$\downarrow$
1066		3878
$\uparrow$		$\downarrow$
2521		7528
$\uparrow$		$\downarrow$
3536		6409
$\uparrow$		$\downarrow$
5620		4177
$\uparrow$		$\downarrow$
7412		7610
$\uparrow$		$\downarrow$
7444		5876
$\uparrow$		$\downarrow$
6260		9140
$\uparrow$		$\downarrow$
2874		9881
$\uparrow$		$\downarrow$
10853		16165
$\uparrow$		$\downarrow$
9738		7947
$\uparrow$		$\downarrow$
9333		8450
$\uparrow$		$\downarrow$
7857		9556
$\uparrow$		$\downarrow$
8136		12161
$\uparrow$		$\downarrow$
$690 \leftarrow 12017 \leftarrow 7976 \leftarrow 7450 \leftarrow 1585 \leftarrow 3617 \leftarrow 4441 \leftarrow 2960 \leftarrow 4432 \leftarrow 5636 \leftarrow 5650 \leftarrow 4163$		

This result made me resolved to find all such loops. First of all I had to decide the upper limit as a starting number. However, any big number will soon get under 9999 on this transformation route (this is not so difficult to prove theoretically), so I looked for loops starting between 1 and 9999.

My friend Professor Narumi and "Ms. YHP 25 mini" programmable calculator assisted me for this work. Loops found were thirteen kinds altogether, and two numbers other than 1 were found to return to themselves at once: 1233   8833

These are thus listed as one-membered loops.

Example for Starting Number	Members in the Loop	Minimum Number in the Loop	Maximum Number in the Loop	
8060	1	(1)	(1)	
3312	1	(1233)	(1233)	
3388	1	(8833)	(8833)	
3750	2	3869	6205	
5158	2	5965	7706	
1883	4	3460	5345	11%
1489	5	1781	7124	
1891	5	3770	8605	
3573	6	4973	7730	
21	10	1268	13441	
1655	14	1946	12437	
2	35	37	14621	31%
1977	56	41	16165	58%

Will someone challenge "Cutting the numbers into every three digits"?

It might be awful. One Japanese addict challenged, and gave up! He wrote to me, "Starting from 2, going through an over-400–membered sidetrack, it entered at last into a 265-membered loop! From 3 to 9, it entered into the same loop too."

1982 and Beyond

In 1982 the *Journal of Recreational Mathematics* published a note by Emrehan Halici on play with the number 1982. Here are some of his results:

Representing 1982 using groups 1, 9, 8, and 2 in order:

$1982 = (1982) + (1 + 9 - 8 - 2)$
$1982 = (19 \times 8^2) + (1 \times 9 \times 8^2) + (19 \times (8 + 2))$
$1982 = (19 \times 82) + (19 \times 8 \times 2) + (19 - 8)^2 - (1 + 9 - 8) \div 2$

Representing integers from 0 to 25 using 1, 9, 8, and 2 in order:

$0 = -1 - 9 + 8 + 2$ $13 = (1 \times 9) + 8 \div 2$

$1 = (1 + 9) \div (8 + 2)$ $14 = -1 + 9 + 8 - 2$

$2 = 1 - 9 + 8 + 2$ $15 = 1 \times 9 + 8 - 2$

$3 = 1 \times (9 - 8) + 2$ $16 = 1 + 9 + 8 - 2$

$4 = 1 + 9 - 8 + 2$ $17 = 1^9 + 8 \times 2$

$5 = 1 \times 9 - 8 \div 2$ $18 = -1 + 9 + 8 + 2$

$6 = 1 + 9 - 8 \div 2$ $19 = 1 \times 9 + 8 + 2$

$7 = 1^9 + 8 - 2$ $20 = 1 + 9 + 8 + 2$

$8 = (-1 + 9 + 8) \div 2$ $21 = -1 + \sqrt{9} \times 8 - 2$

$9 = (1 + 9 + 8) \div 2$ $22 = (1 \times \sqrt{9} + 8) \times 2$

$10 = (-1) \times (\sqrt{9} - 8) \times 2$ $23 = 1 + \sqrt{9} \times 8 - 2$

$11 = 1^9 + 8 + 2$ $24 = -1 + 9 + 8 \times 2$

$12 = -1 + 9 + 8 \div 2$ $25 = -1 + \sqrt{9} \times 8 + 2$

Representing 1982 using integers from 1 to 9 in order:

$$1982 = 1 - 2 + 345 \times 6 - 78 - 9$$
$$1982 = 9 \times (8 + 7) - 6 + 5 + 43^2 - 1$$
$$1982 = 1 - 2 + 3 - 456 - 7 + 8987 - 6543 - 2 + 1$$
$$1982 = 987 + 654 + 3 \times 2 + 1 - 2 + 3 - 456 + 789$$
$$1982 = \frac{9876 + (5 \times 4 - 3) \times 2 \times 1}{9 - 8 + 7 - 6 + 5 - 4 + 3 - 2 + 1}$$

Representing 1982, using powers:

$$1982 = (1^9 - 2^8 + 3^7 - 4^6 + 5^5 + 6^4 - 7^3 + 8^2 + 9^1)$$
$$- (1 - 2 + 3 - 4 + 5 - 6 + 7 - 8 + 9)$$

Halici's play with 1982 led me to wonder whether any year could be dissected and recombined in a similar way. I chose 1937, the year I was born, and used the same constraints as Halici. Here is one possibility using the digits 1, 9, 3, and 7 in order:

$$1937 = (1937) - (1 + 9 - 3 - 7)$$

Using 1, 9, 3, 7 in order, here are some simple results:

$$2 = 1 - 9 + 3 + 7$$
$$4 = -1 + 9 + 3 - 7$$
$$6 = 1 + 9 + 3 - 7$$

I am still playing with 1937 and trying to use its integers to generate all the integers from 1 to 9.

Constructing 100

How many ways can you construct 100 using $+$, $-$, $\times$, $\div$ and the digits from 0 to 9? Here are some answers:

$$100 = 1 + 2 + 3 + 4 + 5 + 6 + 7 + (8 \times 9)$$
$$100 = 12 + 3 - 4 + 5 + 67 + 8 + 9$$

And a backward version:

$$100 = 98 - 76 + 54 + 3 + 21$$

Here are a few more constructions to try by inserting $+$'s or $-$'s between the numbers or groups of the numbers:

$$1 \quad 2 \quad 3 \quad 4 \quad 5 \quad = \quad 6 \quad 7 \quad 8 \quad 9 \quad 0$$
$$1 \quad 3 \quad 5 \quad 7 \quad 9 \quad = \quad 2 \quad 4 \quad 6 \quad 8 \quad 0$$
$$1 \quad 2 \quad 3 \quad 4 \quad 5 \quad 6 \quad 7 \quad 8 \quad 9 \quad = \quad 0$$

I find this kind of exercise a pleasant way to pass a plane or bus trip. I created the following simple game so that similar explorations can be done by several people together.

1 to 6

"1 to 6" is a simple arithmetic game involving adding, subtracting, multiplying, and dividing the numbers 1, 2, 3, 4, 5, and 6. It can be played with paper and pencil. You begin by writing down the following on a piece of paper:

to use: 1 2 3 4 5 6   and $+ + - - \times \times \div \div$
for answers: 0 1 2 3 4 5 6

There are a number of challenges in the game, which can involve any number of people or be played alone. One challenge is to pick a number from the answer set 0, 1, 2, 3, 4, 5, 6 or any combination of numbers in the set, such as 12, 34, 506. This is the target. The goal is to use up as many of the numbers and operations in the "to use" set as you can to reach the target. For example, if the target were 25, here is one way it could be reached:

$$(5 \times 4) + 3 + 2 = 25$$

The solution used up 7 of the 14 allowable symbols.

$$(6 \times 5) - (4 + 3 - 2) = 25$$

This solution used up 9 symbols. In a game context, the score one gets can be the number of symbols used up.

The game itself is simple and is a fun way of fiddling around with numbers. However, other questions can be explored that provide more interesting challenges.

How many equations can you make from the "to use" pool that yield numbers constructed from the answer pool and use the symbols $+$, $-$, $\div$, and $\times$?

What is the smallest number it can be done for? How do you know?

What is the largest?

Which of the numbers in the answer pool cannot be attained by any equation allowable in the game?

What is the smallest? The largest? How many are there?

This leads to the question of how many numbers can be constructed from the number pool and what percentage of them can be generated from the allowable symbols.

Playing with a game like this gets one to feel the character of different numbers and become facile with their relationship to each other. Play a bit with this tiny palette. If you want to expand it, add 7, 8, and 9; increase or decrease the number of each operation ($+$, $-$, $\times$, $\div$) allowed; add new operations, such as square roots and exponents.

If you really want to challenge yourself, try this version in which the equations and target numbers have to be constructed in base 3 arithmetic.

Base 3 arithmetic has only three symbols: 0, 1, and 2. Here is what the numbers from 0 to 10 in our base 10 number system would look like in base 3:

Base 10	Base 3
0	0
1	1
2	2
3	10
4	11
5	12
6	20
7	21
8	22
9	100
10	101

The trick to understanding different base number systems is understanding when and why you add a new column. The answer is that you add a new column when you run out of symbols and have to repeat the ones you are restricted to.

Our everyday number system is a base 10 system that is limited to the symbols 0, 1, 2, 3, 4, 5, 6, 7, 8, and 9. When we get up to 9, we run out of symbols, so we start again, combining symbols: 10, 11, 12, 13, 14, 15, 16, 17, 18, 19.

Notice that we used all the digits we could with a 1 in the first place, so we have run out again. Then we go on to the next symbol in the first place and begin all over again in the second place: 20, 21, 22, 23, 24, 25, 26, 27, 28, 29.

By the time we get to 99, all the two-place number combinations using the symbols 0 to 9 have been used and so we have to add another column, which is what 100 does.

The point is to try to use the symbols chosen to represent quantity in the most efficient and economic way. Each new column in any base system is started because all of the possible combinations of the symbols in that base that can be represented in fewer columns have been exhausted.

For example, compare base 2 and base 5 to the base 10 and 3 systems already presented and complete the chart for 11 to 15 yourself:

Base 10	Base 3	Base 2	Base 5
0	0	0	0
1	1	1	1
2	2	10	2
3	10	11	3
4	11	100	4
5	12	101	10
6	20	110	11
7	21	111	12
8	22	1,000	13
9	100	1,001	14
10	101	1,010	20
11			
12			
13			
14			
15			

If you want to know more about the mathematics of different base systems, consult any junior high or high school mathematics textbook. If you have a feel for how different bases work, whether you know the specific mathematics or not, try this game using the base 3 number system.

You will end up with a deeper understanding of the notion of establishing a base for a number system than if you just read about it.

Permitted symbols: 0, 1, 2   =, −, +

Target answer to be chosen from the following symbols:

0000000000011111111112222222222

Sample challenges:

$$? + ? = 2{,}112$$
$$? + ? - ? = 2{,}020$$
$$? + ? + ? = 12{,}121$$

This same challenge using base 2 or base 16 (hexadecimal) systems is very useful for people who want to learn how to do assembly- and machine-language computer programming.

Classes of Numbers

Number theorists study, among other things, classes of numbers that have shared properties. The simplest classes that come to mind are the even numbers and the odd numbers. However, there are classes that have more complex characteristics and all of whose members may not yet have been discovered. For some classes, it is not even known whether they contain an infinite or finite number of members. Two such classes are "perfect numbers" and "amicable numbers."

Perfect Numbers

A *perfect number* is one that is equal to the sum of all of its factors or divisors except itself. The smallest perfect number is 6. It has as integer divisors 1, 2, and 3, which add up to 6.

If the divisors add up to less than a given number, it is said to be *imperfect* or *defective*. Since 4 has as integer divisors 1 and 2, which add up to 3, it is imperfect.

If the divisors add up to more than a number, it is called *overperfect* or *abundant*. The number 12 has as divisors 1, 2, 3, 4, and 6, which add up to 16; hence, it is overperfect.

See how many perfect, imperfect, and overperfect numbers there are between 1 and 25 or 50 and 100. Do the proportions of perfect to imperfect and overperfect numbers change or remain pretty much the same as you try out more numbers?

A little experimentation should show you that perfect numbers are pretty rare. In fact, the first five perfect numbers are 6, 28, 496, 8,128, and 33,550,336. Fewer than twenty perfect numbers have been found, and they have all been even. It is not known how many perfect numbers there are, and—unless you have a lot of free time on a supercomputer—I'd suggest that you don't try to get to the tenth perfect number.

Amicable Numbers

Two numbers are said to be amicable when the sum of the divisors of the first gives the second, and the sum of the divisors of the second gives the first.

This is not as complex as it sounds. Two such numbers are 220 and 284.

Number	Divisors	Sum of Divisors
220	1, 2, 4, 5, 10, 11, 20, 22, 44, 55, 110	284
284	1, 2, 4, 71, 142	220

For a long time, these were the only two known. In 1636, Pierre de Fermat discovered a second pair: 17,296 and 18,416. In 1866, Paganini found 1,184 and 1,210 to be amicable. Since then, other pairs have been found, but all are very large.

Prime Numbers

Prime numbers are much easier to discover than amicable or perfect numbers, and a lot more is known about them. A *prime number* is one that has as its only divisors 1 and itself. The only even prime number is 2, since every other even number is divisible by 2 by definition. (1 is not prime by convention.) A number that is not prime is called *composite*. Look over the first twelve numbers and determine for yourself how many primes and composites there are:

1: unique   2: prime   3: prime   4: ?   5: ?   6: ?
7: ?   8: ?   9: ?   10: ?   11: ?   12: ?

In the third century B.C., Euclid devised a very simple proof showing that there were an infinite number of primes. Here's a version of it:

If P is any prime number, one can always find another prime number Q that is bigger than P in the following way:

First, construct the number P-factorial (written $P!$). This number consists of P times all of the integers smaller than it. For example:

$$5! = 5 \times 4 \times 3 \times 2 \times 1 = 120$$

Now, for any prime number P, consider the number $P! + 1$. This number is not divisible by P or any number less than P by the way it was constructed. That implies either that it is not divisible at all and therefore is a prime number itself, or that it is divisible by a prime number that lies between P and $P! + 1$. Thus, either $P! + 1$ is a prime number or some number between P and $P! + 1$ is a prime, proving that there is a prime number greater than P.

If you do not follow this proof, then go over it again slowly and use simple examples to illustrate the structure of the proof. It is very helpful, when you are thinking mathematically, to use actual cases to illustrate complex or sophisticated proofs. Here's an example for this proof:

Begin with a prime, say 7, and construct $7! + 1$:

$$7! + 1 = (7 \times 6 \times 5 \times 4 \times 3 \times 2 \times 1) + 1 = 5{,}041$$

which cannot be divided evenly by 2, 3, 4, 5, 6, or 7. Therefore, either nothing other than 1 and itself divides it, or some prime number greater than 7 and less than 5,041 divides it. In either case, the argument shows that there is a prime number greater than 7.

Notice that this proof shows the existence of a prime number greater than 7 *but does not tell what it is.* There is still no general way of discovering, given any prime number P, what the next prime number is, though we know there is a next one. However, there is a method developed by the Greek mathematician Eratosthenes of Alexandria (276–195 B.C.) for determining all of the prime numbers up to a given number. It is called the Sieve of Eratosthenes because it provides a procedure to sift out all of the nonprime (composite) numbers and leave only primes behind. To explore this method for the numbers from 1 to 100, make a copy of the chart below. You'll see that there are twenty-five primes between 1 and 100. How many do you think there will be between 1 and 200? 500? 1,000? If you have the patience, enlarge the chart and, using the sieve method, you'll get the answers quickly.

1	2	3	4	5	6	7	8	9	10
11	12	13	14	15	16	17	18	19	20
21	22	23	24	25	26	27	28	29	30
31	32	33	34	35	36	37	38	39	40
41	42	43	44	45	46	47	48	49	50
51	52	53	54	55	56	57	58	59	60
61	62	63	64	65	66	67	68	69	70
71	72	73	74	75	76	77	78	79	80
81	82	83	84	85	86	87	88	89	90
91	92	93	94	95	96	97	98	99	100

Look at 1, the first integer. Does it fit the definition of a prime number? Its factors are 1 and itself. However, because of the uniqueness of 1 and its factors, it is accepted as neither prime nor composite.

The next number in our chart is 2. It fits the definition of a prime number. The factors of 2 are 1 and itself. Since it is prime, draw a square around it. We will draw squares around all prime numbers and cross out all composites.

If a number is divisible by 2, is it a prime or composite number? If a number is divisible by 2, then 2 is a factor of that number. With the exception of 2, no number with 2 for a factor can be a prime number. Since we want to cross out all composite numbers, we will begin by crossing out all numbers divisible by 2. At this point your sieve should look something like this:

~~1~~	2	3	~~4~~	5	~~6~~	7	~~8~~	9	~~10~~
11	~~12~~	13	~~14~~	15	~~16~~	17	~~18~~	19	~~20~~
21	~~22~~	23	~~24~~	25	~~26~~	27	~~28~~	29	~~30~~
31	~~32~~	33	~~34~~	35	~~36~~	37	~~38~~	39	~~40~~
41	~~42~~	43	~~44~~	45	~~46~~	47	~~48~~	49	~~50~~
51	~~52~~	53	~~54~~	55	~~56~~	57	~~58~~	59	~~60~~
61	~~62~~	63	~~64~~	65	~~66~~	67	~~68~~	69	~~70~~
71	~~72~~	73	~~74~~	75	~~76~~	77	~~78~~	79	~~80~~
81	~~82~~	83	~~84~~	85	~~86~~	87	~~88~~	89	~~90~~
91	~~92~~	93	~~94~~	95	~~96~~	97	~~98~~	99	~~100~~

What is the first number crossed out by using the prime number 2? Keep this in mind. We shall refer to it later.

The next number in our chart is 3. Is it prime? Scratch out every number divisible by 3 (except for 3 itself) that is not already scratched out. Why are these numbers not prime? Keep in mind the first number scratched out when using 3.

The next number not scratched out is 5, which is a prime. What is the first number not scratched out that is divisible by 5? Let us make a chart in which we record some pertinent information. List the prime numbers 2, 3, and 5, and the first number crossed out by each. What is the relationship between each prime number and the first number crossed out by that prime? Use this bit of insight for making a prediction. The next prime number in the chart is 7. What prediction will you make about the first number crossed out by using 7?

Prime Number	First Number Crossed Out
2	4
3	9
5	25

If you made the appropriate generalization, you detected that the first number crossed out by a prime number is the prime times itself (the prime squared). The next prime number that appears on our chart is 11. Since the first number to be scratched out by 11 (11×11) is not on the chart, we can assume we have crossed out all composites and that only primes remain. We have crossed out all multiples of each of the prime numbers 2, 3, 5, and 7. The numbers remaining are not multiples of any number other than 1 and themselves; therefore, they must be prime.

If you crossed out correctly, this is what your chart should look like:

The Sieve of Eratosthenes
Giving the Primes Less than 100

1̶	2	3	4̶	5	6̶	7	8̶	9̶	1̶0̶
11	1̶2̶	13	1̶4̶	1̶5̶	1̶6̶	17	1̶8̶	19	2̶0̶
2̶1̶	2̶2̶	23	2̶4̶	2̶5̶	2̶6̶	2̶7̶	2̶8̶	29	3̶0̶
31	3̶2̶	3̶3̶	3̶4̶	3̶5̶	3̶6̶	37	3̶8̶	3̶9̶	4̶0̶
41	4̶2̶	43	4̶4̶	4̶5̶	4̶6̶	47	4̶8̶	4̶9̶	5̶0̶
5̶1̶	5̶2̶	53	5̶4̶	5̶5̶	5̶6̶	5̶7̶	5̶8̶	59	6̶0̶
61	6̶2̶	6̶3̶	6̶4̶	6̶5̶	6̶6̶	67	6̶8̶	6̶9̶	7̶0̶
71	7̶2̶	73	7̶4̶	7̶5̶	7̶6̶	7̶7̶	7̶8̶	79	8̶0̶
8̶1̶	8̶2̶	83	8̶4̶	8̶5̶	8̶6̶	8̶7̶	8̶8̶	89	9̶0̶
9̶1̶	9̶2̶	9̶3̶	9̶4̶	9̶5̶	9̶6̶	97	9̶8̶	9̶9̶	1̶0̶0̶

Here are a few experiments to try out once you've generated a list of primes:

How many equations can you get of the form

prime + prime = prime? (Example: $2 + 5 = 7$)

How many can you find of the form

prime × prime = prime? (Are there any?)

Can you take a prime and, using $+$, $-$, $\times$, and $\div$, construct it from a combination of other primes? For example, using the first five primes, 2, 3, 5, 7, and 11, can you make the twenty-fifth, which is 97?

Finally, here is a bit of prime trivia. These are the smallest and largest primes with *n* digits, where *n* = 1 to 20:

n	Smallest Prime with n Digits	Largest Prime with n Digits
1	2	7
2	11	97
3	101	997
4	1009	9973
5	10007	99991
6	100003	999983
7	1000003	9999991
8	10000019	99999989
9	100000007	999999937
10	1000000007	9999999967
11	1000000019	99999999977
12	100000000003	999999999989
13	1000000000039	9999999999971
14	1000000000037	99999999999973
15	100000000000031	999999999999989
16	100000000000037	9999999999999937
17	1000000000000061	99999999999999997
18	10000000000000003	999999999999999989
19	10000000000000003	9999999999999999961
20	1000000000000000051	99999999999999999989

Make Your Own Numbers

You can name a class of numbers after yourself. Just find a way to define the class and do some exploration of it. Perhaps someone else has defined the same class. Then you might be a footnote, but given that the number of integers is infinite, there's lots of room to play. Here are two examples of people who named numbers after themselves.

The Duffinian Numbers*
L. Richard Duffy
Cambridge, Massachusetts

It often turns out that much fun can be had by defining new classes of numbers or other mathematical objects, and investigating their resulting properties and relations. This article describes such a venture into the elementary theory of numbers.

We define such a class as follows: A positive composite integer will be called "Duffinian" if the sum of its factors other than itself is not divisible by

*Journal of Recreational Mathematics 12:2 (1979–80).

any of those factors (except 1). The number 1 and the prime numbers are excluded from this class since they have no factors other than 1 and themselves.

To illustrate this definition, take the number 36, whose proper divisors are 1, 2, 3, 4, 6, 9, 12, and 18. None of these (except 1) evenly divides their sum 55; therefore 36 is Duffinian.

The first hundred Duffinian numbers are:

4	8	9	16	21	25	27	32	35	36
39	49	50	55	57	63	64	65	75	77
81	85	93	98	100	111	115	119	121	125
128	129	133	143	144	155	161	169	171	175
183	185	187	189	201	203	205	209	215	217
219	221	225	235	237	242	243	245	247	253
256	259	265	275	279	289	291	299	301	305
309	319	323	324	325	327	329	333	335	338
341	343	351	355	361	363	365	371	377	381
385	387	391	392	399	400	403	407	413	415

One of the first noticeable facts about Duffinian numbers is that most squares and cubes are included (14^2 and 6^3 are the only ones missing from the list).

The Kaprekar Numbers[*]
D. R. Kaprekar
Devlali, India

Numbers like $45^2 = 2025$ (where $20 + 25 = 45$) or $297^2 = 88209$ (where $88 + 209 = 297$) are called Kaprekar numbers. The numbers listed below were discovered by the author some forty years ago, plus many others having a similar property.

1	9		
45	55		
297	703		
2,223	7,777		
2,728	7,272	(Note that all pairs add up	
4,950	5,050	to a power of 10.)	
04,879	95,121		
17,344	82,656		
22,222	77,778		
005,292	994,708	329,967	670,033
038,962	961,038	351,352	648,648
142,857	857,143	356,643	643,357
148,149	851,851	390,313	609,687
187,110	812,890	461,539	538,461
208,495	791,505	466,830	533,170
318,682	681,318	499,500	500,500

*Journal of Recreational Mathematics 13:2 (1980–81).

The smallest number of ten digits having the property above is 1111111111. Its square is 1234567900987654321 and 123456790 + 0987654321 = 1111111111. Other large Kaprekar numbers are 5555555555556 and 22222222222222.

Here are several classes of numbers you might enjoy exploring:

The set of numbers that are structurally symmetrical—that is, numbers such as 2002 and 34455443, which can be divided into two equal numbers of digits that mirror each other (20 and 02; 3445 and 5443). We might call these mathematical palindromes.

The set of numbers that can be divided evenly by the sum of their digits. Some such numbers are 21 (the sum is 3, and 21 ÷ 3 = 7) and 110 (the sum is 2, and 110 ÷ 2 = 55). Numbers such as 25 and 113 are not in the set.

The set of numbers whose digits, when multiplied together, yield the original number. Can you find one?

The set of numbers that have only one divisor other than themselves and 1. One such number is 25, the divisor being 5.

The set of numbers constructed according to a particular rule you make up, such as this one: Pick a beginning number. The next number is that number times the sum of its digits. For example, beginning with 12, here are the first members of the sequence:

$$12, \quad 36\,(12 \times 3), \quad 324\,(36 \times 9), \quad 2{,}916\,(324 \times 9)$$

There is no limit to the number of ways it is possible to choose a set of numbers to explore. Here are some questions you might want to ask once you have chosen such a set:

What is the relationship among the differences between consecutive numbers in your set?

Are all the numbers even, odd, sums of primes, symmetrical, divisors of each other, etcetera?

Are there principles other than the one you used that will generate exactly the same set of numbers?

What properties can be discovered when you add or multiply consecutive members of your sequence?

Number Sequences

Here are a few patterned sequences of numbers:

(a) 2, 4, 6, 8, 10, 12, 14, 16, 18, 20, . . .
(b) 2, 4, 8, 16, 32, 64, 128, 256, . . .
(c) 1, 1, 2, 3, 5, 8, 13, 21, 34, 55, 89, . . .
(d) 1, 5, 6, 11, 17, 28, 45, 73, 118, . . .

You have probably encountered number sequences in school or on different IQ and aptitude tests. Usually the challenge is to fill in the next number in the sequence. Thus, in the above examples:

(a) The next number is 22, as the sequence increases by 2 at every step.

(b) The next number here is 512, as the sequence proceeds by powers of 2; that is, from 2 to 2×2, $2 \times 2 \times 2$, $2 \times 2 \times 2 \times 2$, etcetera.

(c) In this sequence, the pattern may be a little more difficult to detect. Notice that the first two numbers are 1 and 1, and the third is 2, which = 1 + 1. The next number is 3, which is 2 + 1. The one after that is 5, which is 3 + 2. The next term in this sequence, which is called a Fibonacci sequence, is formed by adding the preceding two terms. Therefore, the number after 89 would be 55 + 89 = 144.

(d) This is a Fibonacci sequence beginning with 1 and 5. The number after 118 would therefore be 73 + 118 = 191.

Fibonacci sequences represent some very interesting growth patterns in nature. Lorraine Mottershead's wonderful *Sources of Mathematical Discovery* shows how a numerical relation can be used to understand the structure of some beautiful patterns in the world of plants and animals. I'd like to share this edited version of her section on Fibonacci sequences with you.

This sequence is found by finding the sum of two consecutive terms to give the next term. Thus 1 + 1 = 2, 1 + 2 = 3, 2 + 3 = 5, and so on.

1 1 2 3 5 8 13 . . .

This sequence of numbers owes its name to the great Italian mathematician Leonardo da Pisa (often called Fibonacci, a contraction from "Filius Bonacci," meaning son of Bonacci), who was born in Pisa between 1170 and 1175, and lived until 1230. The construction of the famous Leaning Tower was begun during his lifetime, although it was not completed for nearly two centuries.

He was educated at Bugia and traveled about the Mediterranean collecting information about mathematics. In 1202 he returned to Pisa and published *Liber Abaci,* a book that established the introduction of the Arabic notation in Europe and provided a foundation for future development in arithmetic and algebra. It discussed such topics as the basic operations (multiplication, addition, subtraction, and division), fractions, prices of goods, bartering, problem solving, and the square root, and also mentioned various methods of counting—Arabic, the abacus, and finger reckoning.

Fibonacci posed this problem in *Liber Abaci:*

A pair of rabbits one month old are too young to produce more rabbits, but suppose that in their second month and every month thereafter they produce a new pair. If each new pair of rabbits does the same, and none of the rabbits dies, how many pairs of rabbits will there be at the beginning of each month?

Another one says:

Suppose a cow which first calved when in her second year brings forth a female calf every year, and each she-calf, like her mother, will start calving in her second year and will bring forth a female calf every year—how many calves will have sprung from the original cow and all her descendents in twenty-five years? (*Answer:* 121, 392.)

Both the solutions rely on Fibonacci numbers of the sequence beginning 1, 1.

Fibonacci Sequence Tricks

Impress your friends with mental arithmetic.

1 1 2 3 5 8 13 21 34 55 89 144 233 377 610 987 1,597 2,584

Tell your friend to cut off the sequence at any number and you will add up the preceding numbers (and the cut-off number) mentally!

If 144 is the cut-off, your answer is 376. If 610 is the cut-off point, you say the answer is 1,596.

Can you see how to obtain your answers?

The next trick involves adding, almost instantly, any ten numbers of a Fibonacci sequence.

Ask a friend to write down any two Fibonacci numbers, one below the other, and to add them together to form a third line. Add this line to the one above, to make a fourth line and so on, until there are ten numbers in a vertical column.

You keep your back turned the whole time. After the ten numbers are written, you turn around, draw a line below the column, and quickly write the total. The secret is to multiply the fourth number from the bottom by 11.

Fibonacci in Nature

This magnificent shell is the silent toil of a mollusk which is seldom seen alive. As it grows, the animal secretes partitions within its expanding pearly shell, creating a series of ever larger rooms. By varying the gas content of the abandoned chambers, it changes its buoyancy and dives as deep as two thousand feet at night. Through a tube connected to its body, the nautilus fills the shell chambers with gases so that it will rise in the water and then reabsorbs the gases to sink. Using its muscular funnel, it jets horizontally while feeding with its many tentacles near coral reefs during the day. A cephalopod ("head-foot"), the most highly developed of mollusks, the once abundant chambered nautilus stopped evolving eons ago. Today, the western Pacific harbors the last four species of this living fossil.

Trace this spiral, clearly marking the twenty-five points. Join each point to the twenty-four others.

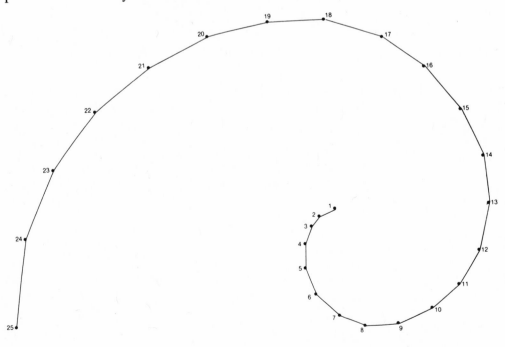

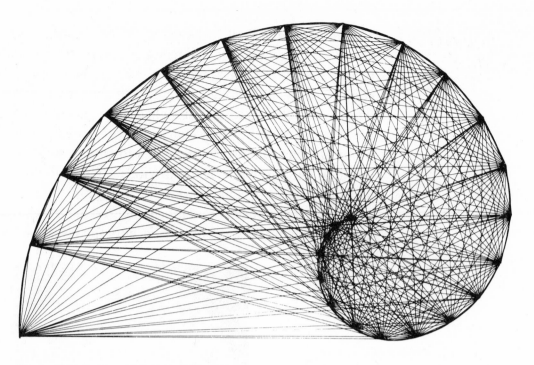

Your finished result should be a "mystic nautilus."

Using a Number Grid to Explore Patterns

A useful device for exploring number patterns is this simple chart containing the numbers from 1 to 100. It is a version of the one used for the Sieve of Eratosthenes. If possible, make a number of copies of the chart to use for pattern exploration.

1	2	3	4	5	6	7	8	9	10
11	12	13	14	15	16	17	18	19	20
21	22	23	24	25	26	27	28	29	30
31	32	33	34	35	36	37	38	39	40
41	42	43	44	45	46	47	48	49	50
51	52	53	54	55	56	57	58	59	60
61	62	63	64	65	66	67	68	69	70
71	72	73	74	75	76	77	78	79	80
81	82	83	84	85	86	87	88	89	90
91	92	93	94	95	96	97	98	99	100

One way to begin to explore patterns on the grid is to draw diagonal lines and try to figure out a pattern that accounts for each of the numbers on each line. For example, here are four lines. What patterns do they represent? Do you notice any similarities among the patterns?

A		B	C						D
1	2	3	4	5	6	7	8	9	10
11	12	13	14	15	16	17	18	19	20
21	22	23	24	25	26	27	28	29	30
31	32	33	34	35	36	37	38	39	40
41	42	43	44	45	46	47	48	49	50
51	52	53	54	55	56	57	58	59	60
61	62	63	64	65	66	67	68	69	70
71	72	73	74	75	76	77	78	79	80
81	82	83	84	85	86	87	88	89	90
91	92	93	94	95	96	97	98	99	100

The pattern traced by line A can be represented as +11. The same is true for line B. Lines C and D represent +9 patterns. Is it true that all diagonal patterns are +9 or +11? If so, why?

Now, instead of drawing lines, shade in numbers to represent patterns. As you saw in the section on Fibonacci sequences, patterns can often be represented by pictures. Here for instance is a picture of a Fibonacci sequence (the 1, 1).

1	2	3	4	5	6	7	8	9	10
11	12	13	14	15	16	17	18	19	20
21	22	23	24	25	26	27	28	29	30
31	32	33	34	35	36	37	38	39	40
41	42	43	44	45	46	47	48	49	50
51	52	53	54	55	56	57	58	59	60
61	62	63	64	65	66	67	68	69	70
71	72	73	74	75	76	77	78	79	80
81	82	83	84	85	86	87	88	89	90
91	92	93	94	95	96	97	98	99	100

You can create puzzles for your friends by coloring pattern squares on the number grid and then transferring them to this blank grid. The goal is to look at the grid without counting and try to figure out the rule for the pattern.

[blank 10×10 grid]

Here are some sequences to color in as a beginning:

• prime numbers
• prime numbers + 1
• add multiples of 3 but begin on square number 4
• add 2 to the first number, 3 to the second, 4 to the third, etcetera
• begin at 100 and subtract first 2, then 3, 4, etcetera.

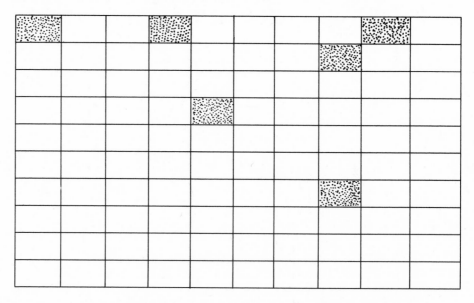

What pattern is this? What would be the next square you'd fill in?

Solution:

    The pattern begins with 1 and then skips 2 spaces to get to 4. Then it skips 4 spaces, getting to 9. The next step skips 8 spaces, arriving at 18. Notice that the differences—2, 4, and 8—are powers of 2. The next power of 2, 2^4, is 16, which will get the pattern to 35. One can guess that the next step would be to skip 2^5 or 32 squares, which is what happens. The pattern, then, is to increase the number of skipped pairs at each step by a power of 2. The general pattern can be described in the following way: at the nth step, you skip 2^n squares. This is not easy to see at first, but you'll be surprised to discover how your feel for number patterns grows with practice.

Every book I have written has been enhanced by an almost anonymous individual who reads my text as closely as I ever do and provides useful and very specific comments on the quality of the work. That person is called a copy editor, and I venture that many publishers would produce books that read as if they were typed at random by monkeys chained to typewriters if it were not for copy editors. Beverly Colman, the copy editor of this book, added a bit of number madness to all the helpful suggestions she made about how to smooth out my final draft for publication. Here is her bit of number play—a practical illustration and a demystification of one of the jillions of numbers that are now popping up on consumer products.

Almost all books now have an ISBN (International Standard Book Number) on the copyright page and on the cover. For this book (in hardcover), it will be 0–8052–4022–5. The first 0 tells that the book is in the English language. The next set of numbers (8052) identifies the publisher as Schocken Books. The next set (4022) is the number assigned to your particular book (different for hardcover and paperback), and the last number (5) is the check digit, which will cause the computer to spit out the ISBN if one of the earlier numbers is wrong.

$$0 \quad 8 \quad 0 \quad 5 \quad 2 \quad 4 \quad 0 \quad 2 \quad 2 \quad 5$$
$$9 \quad 8 \quad 7 \quad 6 \quad 5 \quad 4 \quad 3 \quad 2 \quad 1$$

(Ignore the first 0, since we're going to multiply.) Multiply each digit by the one under it. Here, we get

$$72 \quad 0 \quad 35 \quad 12 \quad 20 \quad 0 \quad 0 \quad 6 \quad 4 \quad 5$$

Add these up, and the sum is 154. The sum must be evenly divisible by 11—if not, computers explode. (I understand this is called modulus 11 in computerese.)

Similarly, if you wanted to find out a check digit you didn't know (a computer-generated list of ISBN's is sent to all publishers in the system), you would simply multiply and add all the numbers you do have, and your check digit would have to be (since it is multiplied by 1) the number that would bring you up to the next evenly divisible 11. For example:

$$0 \quad 8 \quad 0 \quad 5 \quad 2 \quad 0 \quad 7 \quad 9 \quad 7 \quad ?$$
$$9 \quad 8 \quad 7 \quad 6 \quad 5 \quad 4 \quad 3 \quad 2 \quad 1$$

The sum of the multiplications is 188, which, divided by 11, gives 17 with 1 left over. To bring that 1 up to 11, the check digit is 10, for which the symbol X is used.

The ISBN system, to consolidate ordering, is now in use in 57 countries. It is used by bookstore chains, large book distributors, university bookstores, and school systems. It has been expanded to include serial magazines and journals, computer software, audio and video tapes, etcetera.

Knots, Maps, and Connections

Really, universally, relations stop nowhere, and the exquisite problem of the artist is eternally but to draw, by a geometry of his own, the circle within which they shall happily *appear* to do so.
—Henry James, preface to *Roderick Hudson*

Knots

Topology is one of the most imaginative branches of modern mathematics. It requires thinking yourself into a world where squares, circles, and triangles are all considered the same kind of object; where size is irrelevant; where stretching and twisting do not change the mathematical nature of an object.

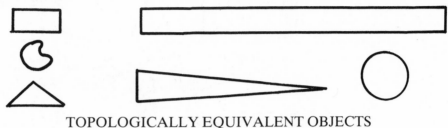

TOPOLOGICALLY EQUIVALENT OBJECTS

It is possible to isolate certain features of objects or structures and study the characteristics they would have if the world were as simple as mathematics. Topology is basically the study of inside, outside, and boundaries. It ranges from the study of the coloring of maps to the analysis of the nature of holes in knots and doughnuts (mathematical ones, of course). It deals with the properties of things that remain unchanged no matter how you twist or stretch them. Below is a simple example. No matter how you twist or stretch the face, the eyes remain inside the boundary and the dot remains outside.

Here are some topologically equivalent forms. Notice that, in the first set, the objects have no holes; in the second set, they have only one hole; and in the third set, two holes. If you can't see this immediately, take a piece of clay and model the figures. Remember that—no matter how you stretch or pinch or dent them—as long as the number of holes stays the same, the objects are topologically equivalent.

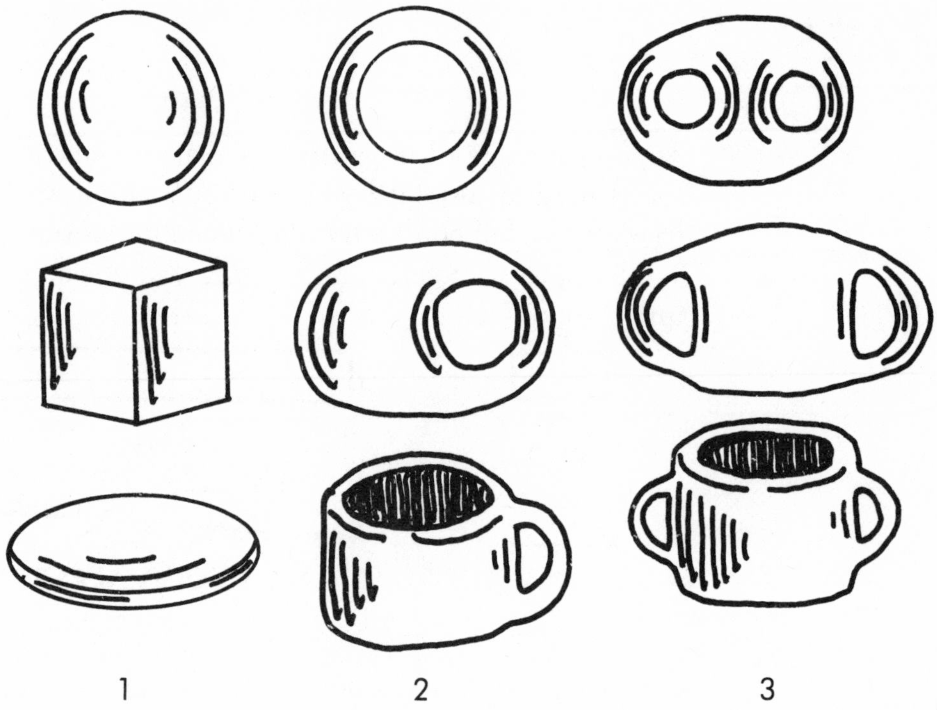

Challenge: From a topological point of view, which object does not belong in the set in each box?

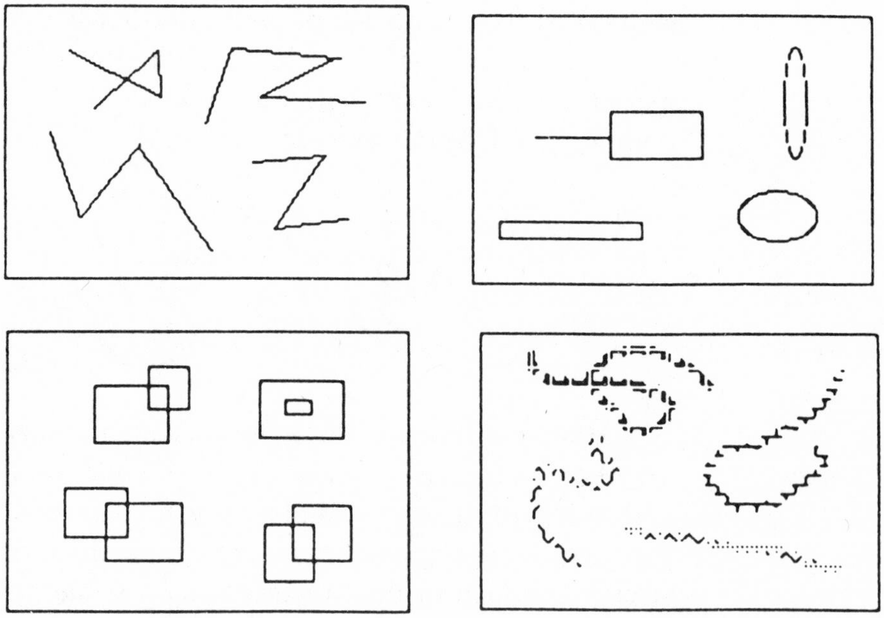

Solution:

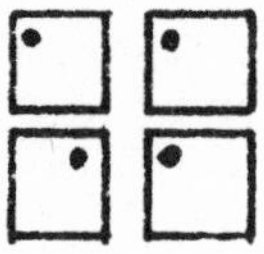

Let's look at the topological puzzlement of knots, which, according to Funk and Wagnall's *Standard Dictionary of Folklore,* play different roles as cultural symbols throughout the world.

To tie a knot is to make something fast, to bind, hold, also to hinder or stop. To untie a knot is to loosen, set free, release. The knot unites, therefore, and binds together; it strengthens love and marriage; it also shuts out evil and binds evil-doers into inaction.

The knot without beginning and without end was one of the symbols of the Hindu Vishnu and of life without beginning and without end. . . .

Everywhere in India a knot is tied in the clothes of bride and bride-groom in marriage ceremonies; . . . Roman marriage ceremonies comprised a whole series of knot-tyings and untyings from the first tying on of the bride's girdle, and her tying the woolen strands on her husband's door-posts, to the final untying of the girdle in the bridal chamber. The love-knot . . . has an ancient and solemn authority. . . .

It is a common world practice to untie all knots during childbirth to facilitate the birth . . . and in some localities the magic of . . . release is enhanced by the freeing of captive birds and animals, untying of domestic animals, etc.

Knots have long been used in the causing and curing of diseases. Seven knots and twice seven knots are especially potent. Nine knots are the worst of evil spells.

Tying up the wind in a knot is part of the old wisdom of northern fishing communities, especially in Lapland, Finland, the Shetlands, Isle of Man, etc. Then untying the knot raises enough wind to fill the sails.

. . . This concept is at least as old as Aeolus, who gave Odysseus the winds tied up in a bag (*Odyssey* x, 19f.).

It is not likely that you have ever encountered a mathematical knot. Most of the knots people tie are not knots from a topological point of view. The following knots are all topologically identical. In fact, the whole string of knots is topologically identical to four straight lines because the ends are not joined together. You can undo them in your mind.

However, here is an undoable knot. It is topologically knotted in that there is no beginning or end to the loop that contains the knot. In the physical world, we make a knot from a piece of rope or string that has two ends. A topological knot exists in imaginary, mathematical space and must be cut to be transformed into a straight piece of string. Here is a constructed picture of what a topological knot might look like:

A topological knot has no seams, no beginning, and no end. It is continuous and self-contained. It was never tied. It is a creation of the imagination, yet, like many constructions of the mind, it can be examined, drawn, and played with as if it actually existed. There are many topological knots in works of art and design:

Needlepoint Pattern by
Albrecht Dürer
(Nuremberg, 1505)

*Knots, Maps, and
Connections*

Topological knots contain a specified number of internal crossings that define their mathematical properties. An internal crossing occurs when a string passes through a loop as in the following illustration:

Create a loop by laying one end of a string over the string:

Pass one of the ends through the loop:

When pulled tight the knot with one crossing looks like this:

If you seal the ends you get a topological knot with one crossing (that is one passage through the loop):

The main problems of knot theory are:

- to decide if a given closed loop is knotted or not
- to decide whether two knots are topologically the same or different
- to list all possible knots.

In the illustrations of knots in this section, a broken line indicates that one strand is under another one. A solid line indicates that it is on top of another one. A simple real-world knot in a string would be represented this way:

A topological knot with one crossing would look like this:

Here is a simple band with no internal crossings:

Below are several examples of a knot with one crossing. They are all topologically equivalent:

The following tangle has no knots and is topologically equivalent to the simple band:

Here are two topologically equivalent knots with two crossings:

Which of these knots have the same number of crossings?

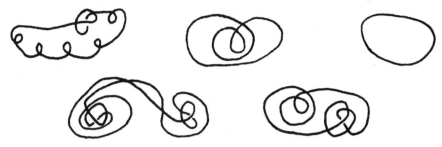

There is a simple trick with a piece of string that will give you a sense of the cross that leads to a true topological knot. If you let go of the ends of the rope in the trick, you no longer have a topological knot, as the ends are untied. Your arms and body are necessary for the approximation to a topological knot with no ends.

Pick up a string by holding the ends of it in your hands and tie a knot in it without letting go of the ends of the string. You probably picked up the string and held it as in the first picture. This is just what you are expected to do. But the directions did not say *how* to pick up the string.

There is a simple solution: Before picking up the string, cross your arms in front of your chest. Now pick up the string at both ends, as in the figure. Just unfold your arms and the knot will form. What you are doing is knotting your arms. When you unfold them, you are transferring the knot to the string topologically.

Now let's take a look at two knots illustrated before. These are the two simplest knots. One is the mirror image of the other. They both have only one crossing, but one is left-handed and the other right-handed. You can't twist them into each other:

The number of crossings in a knot is one of its principal features. Here are knots of four, five, six, and seven crossings. Try to make models of them, using some string. Slip the knots around the string to get a sense of the different ways the same topological structure can look. When you do this, you are topologically distorting equivalent structures—a fancy way of saying you are playing with a structure without changing the relationships of inside and outside, or modifying its boundaries.

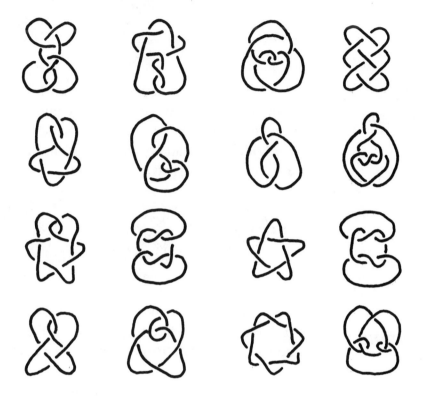

Links are almost knots. Here is a picture of what is called a Borromean link. Notice that no two of the links are joined together, and if one were cut, the three would simply come apart.

There are other examples of unjoined links that adhere as a structure and fall apart with a single cut.

Here are some ways of making and playing with knots. First, four fancy knots, which you can use as decorations. They are taken from R. M. Abraham's *Tricks and Amusements with Coins, Cards, String, Paper and Matches*.

Japanese Fancy Knot

This knot, which is made by four cords, is formed as shown in figure 1. All the parts are drawn up tight to make figure 2. This knot is used in combination with others of the same sort to make sword ornamentations.

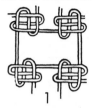

Three-Part Turk's Head

Lay the cord down as in figure 1 and draw loops A and B out on each side as shown: B over its left loop, and A under its right loop. Pass end C under and over, and under and over, as indicated in figure 2, thus making figure 3. Follow the lead around with C and D as many times as you like. Figure 4 shows the finished Turk's head.

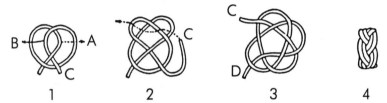

Chinese Fancy Knots

The easiest method of making knots of this kind is to pin the cords down on a cushion or pillow filled with sand. A little practice is required to get the knots symmetrical. Braided blind cord is suitable for making these knots.

Chinese Basket Knot

This knot is rather complicated to make, and can only be done by pinning the cords down to a cushion or by winding them around a number of nails hammered into a board. It is made from two cords A and B, or from one

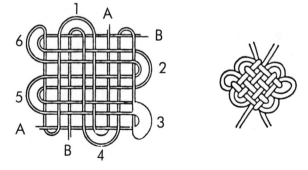

cord doubled in the center. When all the interlacing has been done, loops 1 to 6 are pulled out, forming the finished knot shown.

Below is an example of an Arabic knot pattern used for decoration. How many crossings are there in figure 1?

Notice that figure 3 is built out of repeats of figure 1 (as shown in figure 2). Try to draw this and vary the basic pattern. The easiest way is to use graph paper.

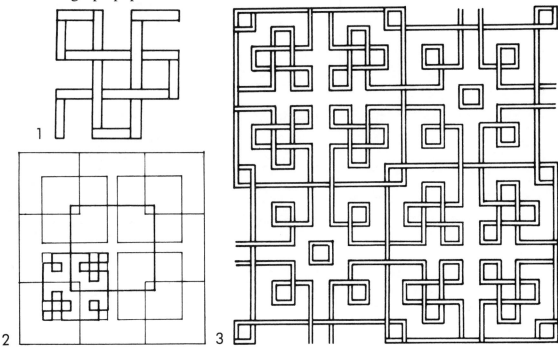

Celtic and Scandinavian art is full of knots such as these:

Here are some diagrams that will help you draw them. By the way, how many crossings are there in the knots illustrated?

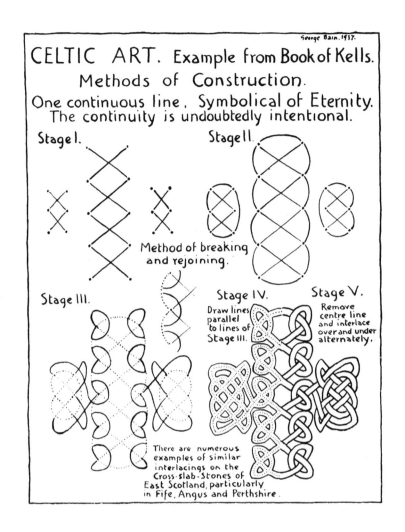

CELTIC ART. Example from Book of Kells.
Methods of Construction.
One continuous line. Symbolical of Eternity.
The continuity is undoubtedly intentional.

George Bain. 1937.

Stage I.

Stage II.

Method of breaking and rejoining.

Stage III.

Stage IV.
Draw lines parallel to lines of Stage III.

Stage V.
Remove centre line and interlace over and under alternately.

There are numerous examples of similar interlacings on the Cross-slab-Stones of East Scotland, particularly in Fife, Angus and Perthshire.

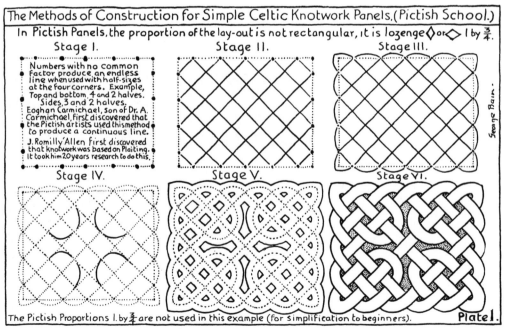

The Methods of Construction for Simple Celtic Knotwork Panels, (Pictish School.)
In Pictish Panels, the proportion of the lay-out is not rectangular, it is lozenge ◇ or ◇ 1 by ¾.

Stage I.
Numbers with no common factor produce an endless line when used with half-sizes at the four corners. Example, Top and bottom, 4 and 2 halves. Sides, 3 and 2 halves.
Eoghan Carmichael, son of Dr. A. Carmichael, first discovered that the Pictish artists used this method to produce a continuous line.
J. Romilly Allen first discovered that knotwork was based on Plaiting. It took him 20 years research to do this.

Stage II.

Stage III.

George Bain.

Stage IV.

Stage V.

Stage VI.

The Pictish Proportions 1. by ¾ are not used in this example (for simplification to beginners).

Plate I.

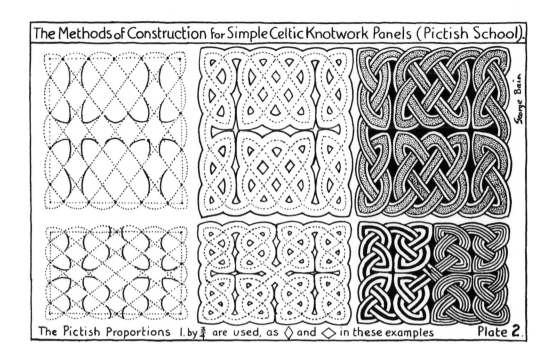

The Methods of Construction for Simple Celtic Knotwork Panels (Pictish School).

The Pictish Proportions 1. by ¾ are used, as ◊ and ◇ in these examples   Plate **2**.

Paper Knots

Paper knot tying can lead to the construction of many regular geometric forms. Try the following knots from Donavan A. Johnson's *Paper Folding for the Mathematics Classroom*. You might even find them useful as Christmas decorations.

SQUARE

Use two strips of paper of the same width. Fold each strip over upon itself to form a loop. Insert an end of one strip into the loop of the other so that the strips interlock. Pull tightly together and cut off the surplus. Why is the polygon a square?

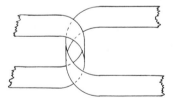
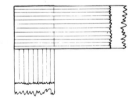

PENTAGON

Use a long strip of paper of constant width. Adding machine tape is a convenient size to use. Tie an overhand knot, like the first knot in tying a shoestring. Tighten and crease flat. Cut the surplus lengths. Unfold and consider the set of trapezoids formed by the creases. How do the trapezoids compare?

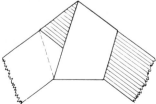

HEXAGON

Use two long strips of paper of equal width. Tie a square knot as shown below on the left. Tuck the ends of each strip into the loop of the other. Tighten and crease flat. Cut the surplus lengths.

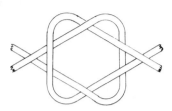
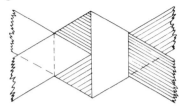

HEPTAGON

Use a long strip of paper of constant width. Tie a knot like that for the pentagon above, but, before tightening, pass the lead strip under the knot and back through the center.

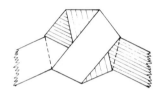

OCTAGON

Use two long strips of paper of the same width. First tie a loose overhand knot with one strip, like that for the pentagon above. The figure below shows this tie with the shaded strip going from 1–2–3–4–5. With the second strip, start at 6, pass over 1–2 and over 3–4. Bend up at 7. Pass under 4–5 and 1–2. Bend up at 9. Pass over 3–4, under 7–8 and 4–5, emerging at 10. Tighten and crease flat. Cut surplus lengths 1, 5, 6, 10.

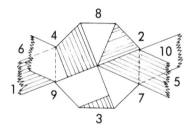

The Möbius Strip

In the mid-nineteenth century the German mathematician and astronomer Augustus Möbius discovered a one-sided strip of paper that has interesting topological features you can experiment with.

Here are some ways of playing with the Möbius strip drawn from Lorraine Mottershead's *Sources of Mathematical Discovery*. But first a limerick that summarizes some of the striking properties of the Möbius strip.

> A mathematician confided
> That a Möbius band is one-sided;
> But you'll get quite a laugh,
> If you cut one in half,
> For it stays in one piece when divided.

To understand what happens when a Möbius strip is cut, it is necessary to carry out the practical experiments yourself and to record the results in a table. It is hard to predict the outcomes!

Cut about eight strips of paper, each about 12″ long and $1\frac{1}{2}$″ wide.

1. Take one of the strips and glue or tape the ends together, making sure there are no twists.
    How many sides and edges has it?
    If it were cut down a center line, what would be formed? What are the properties of these halves?
    This is a simple ring. Now for the Möbius twist.

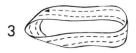

2. Take another strip and make a half-twist (180 degrees) at one end before joining the two ends.
    Now draw a pencil line down the center of the strip, continuing until you come back to where you started.
    Cut along this line. What happens?
    How many half-twists are there in the model now?

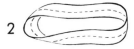

3. Take another Möbius strip and cut along it parallel to an edge and about one-third of the way from the edge.
    Continue cutting until you arrive at your starting point.
    What is the result this time?
    What are the length and width of these loops?

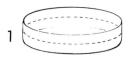

4. Do the above operations again, except that you must cut it one-quarter of the way from an edge.

In what ways is this result similar to or different from the previous one?

Can you guess what the result would be if you cut around the strip one-fifth of the way from an edge?

Repeat steps 2 to 4 on strips with two half-twists (360 degrees), three half-twists (540 degrees), and four half-twists (720 degrees). Summarize your results.

Number of Half-Twists	Center Cut Forms	Description in Words	Sketch	One-Third Cut Forms	One-Quarter Cut Forms
0	Two separate strips	Half as wide, same length as original			
1 (one surface, one edge)	One strip	Half as wide, twice as long			
2 (two sides, two edges)					
3					
4					

Experiment with these fancy versions of the Möbius strip:

Slit Strips

With a long piece of paper, cut a slit before pushing one end through and joining. Extend the slit right around the band.

In a similar manner, push the top end through the slit after giving it a twist toward you, so that when the ends are joined, the top surface is glued to the bottom surface. What happens?

Siamese Möbius Strips

Take a long strip of paper and cut two longitudinal slits. Bring the upper pair of ends together and join with a half-twist so that A joins A[1], and B joins B[1].

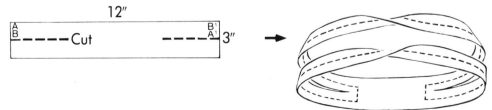

Do the same with the lower slits, but twist in the opposite direction. Then cut along the dotted line.

Hexaflexagons

This dramatic variation of the Möbius strip requires a paper strip that is at least six times as long as it is wide.

First fold the strip to locate the center line CD at one end of the strip.

Fold the strip so that B falls on CD and the resulting crease AE passes through A. What kind of a triangle is ABE?

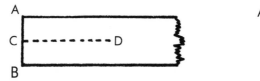

Fold the strip back so that the crease (EG) forms along BE. What kind of a triangle is EGA? Next fold forward along GA, forming another triangle. Continue folding back and forth until ten equilateral triangles have been formed. Cut off the excess of the strip as well as the first right triangle ABE.

Lay the strip in the position shown in the top illustration below right, and number the triangles accordingly.

Turn the strip over and number as shown in the bottom illustration. Be sure that triangle 11 is behind triangle 1. Coloring each triangle or drawing designs on them will add to the attractiveness of the hexaflexagons.

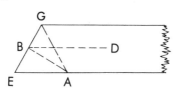

Front

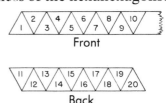
Back

To fold the hexaflexagon, lay the strip flat with the front face up. Fold triangle 1 over triangle 2. Then fold triangle 15 on triangle 14, and triangle 8 on triangle 7. If your folding now gives you the arrangements shown below, glue triangle 1 to 10. If you do not have this arrangement, recheck the directions.

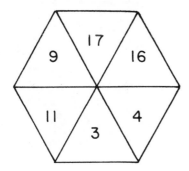

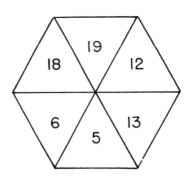

Your hexagon will now open and give you three surfaces or six designs. The designs open easily by folding in the three single edges, forming a three-cornered star and opening out the center.

Finally how about a Möbius strip hat? Show your friends you know what topology is all about by wearing one to all the most fashionable events. Here are instructions on how to crochet your own Möbius hat. They were sent to me by Joan Ross, who is one of the greatest mathematical gamesters I've met.

This delightful article was invented by my friend Lois Kane, a weaver of some note. Lois was trying to make a bag, but a hat is what happened. (I have since tried to knit a Möbius hat, but I have failed. Knitting is very two-dimensional, but crocheting is basically one-dimensional and hence more appropriate to the creation of Möbius strips.) The recipe for a Kane–Möbius hat is as follows:

Crochet a chain between 36″ and 50″ long.

Join the ends of the chain, but make a single half-twist before you do so.

Commence making a single (or double or whatever stitch combination you choose) crochet in each stitch of the chain. You will discover (of course!) that when you get back to where you joined the ends of the chain, you are on the opposite side of the stitch. Continue.

Decrease from time to time so that the hat lies flat.

Eventually the hat opening will get to be the right size for the person who will wear it. When it does, stop.

One final puzzle: When I wanted to measure the starting chain of a hat I had already made, I put a safety pin into the "outer edge" of the hat and measured around, and around, and around. The length seemed much longer than the length I vaguely recalled. Then I laughed as I realized that I had measured right past the pin— because it was inside the hat.

Knots, Maps, and Connections

Map Coloring

Map coloring is a topological matter. No matter how you stretch or shirnk or expand or twist a map, the boundaries of the different regions remain the same. Here's an example of some topological transformations of the map of Spain, Portugal, and France. Notice that the boundaries never change: Portugal never touches France.

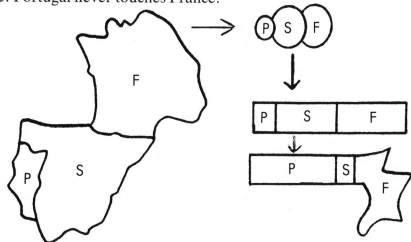

How many colors do you need to color in a map so that no two areas of the same color are touching? Try these maps:

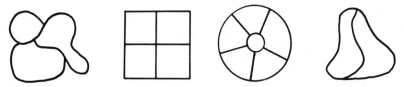

It wasn't until recently that it was proved that you'll never need more than four colors to color any such map that can be drawn on the plane. The proof is extremely long and was done with the aid of a computer. However, map-coloring problems provide fascinating challenges.

Below are several maps. Find the smallest number of colors needed to fill them in so that no boundaries have the same colors.

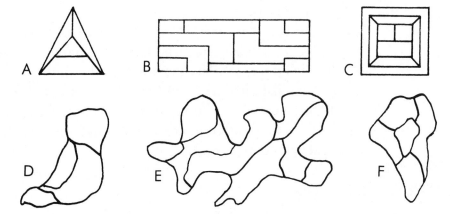

Answers:

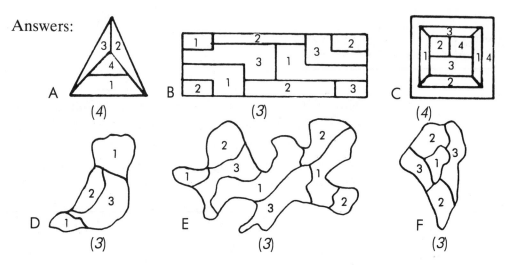

A (4)   B (3)   C (4)

D (3)   E (3)   F (3)

Now make your own maps and color them.

How many colors are needed for coloring these maps so that no two regions with a common border will have the same color? This challenge and the following Two-Color Theorem are taken from *Super Games* by Ivan Moscovich.

The Two-Color Theorem

While four colors are needed for most maps, maps drawn in special ways may not need as many. An extreme case is where the maps are drawn using only straight lines. A little experiment suggests that two colors are then sufficient.

Is this true?

In fact it is, and the proof is quite easy. Add the lines one by one to the map. As each line is added, interchange the two colors on all regions that lie on *one side* of the new line. This makes the colors remain different across old boundaries, and also across the new one, thanks to the interchange of colors. The same proof can be generalized to apply to maps in which the boundaries are either single curves that run right across the whole plane, or closed loops.

All these two-color maps have an *even* number of edges meeting at any junction. This must be true of any map that can be colored with just two colors, because the regions around a junction or corner must be of alternate colors. More than this: it can be proved that any map on the plane can be colored using only two colors if and only if all its junctions have an even number of edges meeting there. This is the Two-Color Theorem.

   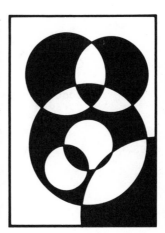

Here's a puzzle for two players, originated by Lewis Carroll:

Player A draws a fictitious map divided into countries (say, ten countries or less).

Player B tries to color it (or mark the countries with names of colors) using as *few* colors as possible, with the restriction that two adjacent countries must have *different* colors (countries that touch at a point, such as X and Y in the illustration below, are not considered adjacent). A map that is colored in this way is said to be "properly" colored.

A's object is to make B use as many colors as possible. With the right map, A can force B to use as many as four colors.

In the illustration below, figures 1 and 2 can be properly colored in two colors, figure 3 in three colors, and figure 4 requires four different colors (see if you can do it). In figure 1, countries X and Y are not adjacent so can be colored with the same color, while X and Z are adja-

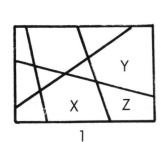 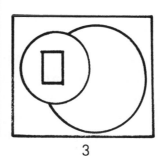  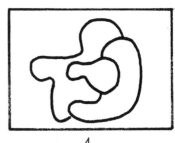

1   2   3   4

cent and must have different colors. Since there are many ways to color the same map, you can give a lot of people the same map and see who can properly color it with the fewest number of colors. The entire map must be colored.

Here are three games that illustrate map coloring in the real world, from *Your Move,* by David L. Silverman.

Monochrome

Two players take turns shading any South American country of their choice, with one restriction. There is only one color available, and since it is traditional among mapmakers never to color neighboring countries alike, the rules prohibit the shading of any country that borders a previously shaded country.

The winner is the player who is able to shade the last country—i.e., who is first able to stymie his opponent.

Solution:

The fact that Brazil borders ten of the thirteen countries of South America, while the two countries with which it has no common border are not adjacent, permits you to win with dispatch.

Shade Brazil. Your opponent is then left with only two choices: Chile or Ecuador. Whichever he shades, you shade the other; the game is over.

Can you guarantee by any other opening? Very likely, but not nearly so quickly. Moreover, the analysis required to determine the winning strategy with any other opening is probably sufficiently complicated to require a digital computer.

Bichrome

In Bichrome the principle of play is identical to that of Monochrome, except that each player has the option of using either of two shades on each move, say red or black. He may shade any Australian province with the proviso that it must not have the same color as any previously shaded province with which it shares a common border.

The object is to stymie your opponent, the winner being the player who makes the last legal move. In this game, your opponent has drawn first move and has chosen to color Victoria black. You have eight different options for your reply. You can shade South Australia or New South Wales red, or you can shade Queensland, Northern Territory, or Western Australia with either of the two colors.

Only one of the eight options will insure you a win.

Solution:

Reduced to a simpler, rectangular map, the Australian provinces show an interesting symmetry that facilitates the solution considerably.

Shade Western Australia red. This puts South Australia out of play and limits your opponent's options to four. Depending on which he chooses, you will stymie him on your next move by shading Northern Territory black or New South Wales red, whichever of the two plays is legal.

Western Australia	Northern Territory	Queensland	New South Wales	Victoria
South Australia				

Had you made any other response to your opponent's opening move, it is simple to verify that in each of the seven cases he would have been able to seize the initiative. It will be a profitable exercise for you to work out your opponent's winning second move in each case. It happens that it always involves shading with the color opposite that used in your response.

Finally, it should be noted that the symmetry of the provincial boundaries dooms the first player to defeat in Australian Bichrome. To the openings of Victoria, New South Wales, or South Australia, you respond with Western Australia, Northern Territory, or Queensland, respectively, and vice versa. In all cases use the opposite color. You can readily verify that these will be winning responses.

Trichrome

This time you are playing the three-color game on a map of thirteen western states. Your opponent started by shading California, and after five moves only two of the three colors have been used (indicated above by numbers).

Normally it would take some involved analysis to determine your optimum move, but your opponent has left you a configuration in which you can assure yourself a win without the necessity of following the numerous branches along which the game might proceed.

Study the map carefully.

Solution:

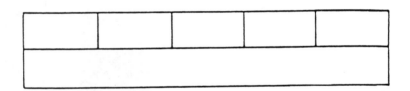

The topological chart above bears a remarkable resemblance to that of the Australian provinces (see preceding game). Moreover, none of these six states can legally be shaded with color 2. Thus, if you can reduce the game to these six states with your opponent required to play first, you will have reduced the game to Australian Bichrome, to which you already know the winning responses.

Your winning move is to shade Oregon with color 3. This makes Nevada unplayable, and your opponent is forced to choose from six losing openings in the equivalent of Australian Bichrome.

The next exploration of map coloring comes from *Mathematics and the Imagination* by Edward Kastner and James Newton. A Dutch mathematician, L. E. J. Brouwer, concocted an example—at first sight wholly unbelievable—of a map of three countries, on which *every single point along the boundary of each country is a meeting place of all three countries.*

Consider the map below.

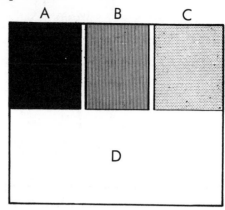

Countries A, B, C are separated by
unoccupied corridors and D is unclaimed land

None of the nations borders on any of its neighbors, and the white unmarked portion of the map is intended to represent unclaimed territory. Country A decides to extend its sphere of influence over the unclaimed land by grabbing a substantial portion. Accordingly, it sends out a corridor that does not touch the land of either of its neighbors, but leaves no point of the remaining, unclaimed land more than one mile from some point of the enlarged country A. It has now spread itself over the map as seen below.

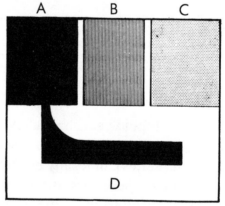

Country B, instead of applying sanctions, decides to grab a share before it is too late. With becoming restraint, as well as with an eye to its neighbors' greater strength, B extends a corridor to within a half-mile of every point of the remaining unclaimed land. This corridor alters the map like this:

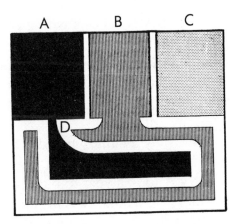

Of course country C will not be left behind. It builds a corridor that approaches within a third of a mile of every point of the remaining unclaimed land but, just as the other two corridors, touches on no country but its own. The new map is shown below.

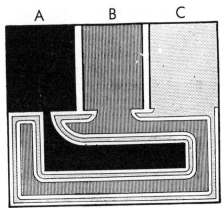

By now everyone should be quite content. On the contrary; this is only the beginning. Country A has the shortest corridor. An intolerable state of affairs! It decides on a new corridor to extend into the remaining territory that shall approach every point of that territory within a quarter of a mile.

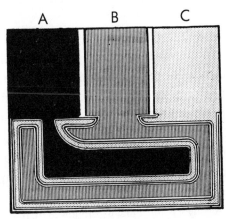

Country B follows with a corridor that approaches each unoccupied point within a fifth of a mile, country C's corridor comes within a sixth of a mile of each unoccupied point, and the merry-go-round goes round. More and more corridors! Never any contact between them, although they continue to come closer and closer, $\frac{1}{7}, \frac{1}{8}, \frac{1}{9}, \ldots \frac{1}{100}, \ldots \frac{1}{1000}, \ldots \frac{1}{1000000}, \ldots \frac{1}{googol},$* $\ldots$ of a mile.

We may assume, in order for this feverish program to be completed in a finite length of time ("Two-Year Plan"), that the first corridor of country A took a year to build, the first corridor of B a half-year, the first corridor of C a quarter-year, the second corridor of country A an eighth of a year, and so on. Each corridor took exactly half as long to build as its immediate predecessor. The total elapsed time then gives rise to the familiar series

$$1 + \frac{1}{2} + \frac{1}{4} + \frac{1}{8} + \frac{1}{16} + \frac{1}{32} + \ldots = 2$$

Thus, at the end of two years, the once unclaimed territory has been entirely occupied, and not a speck of it remains unclaimed. Over each square inch there flies the flag of one of the three countries, either A, B, or C.

What of the new map that is to depict these boundaries? Actually, it is impossible to draw, but suppose we try to conceive what it would look like if it could be drawn. This conceptual map is put together out of pieces of sober mathematics and sheer fancy. For *every single boundary point on the map will be a meeting place, a boundary point, of not two, but of all three countries!*

Connections and Tracings

Graph theory is a very important branch of higher mathematics and yet it can be illustrated by simple mathematical recreations. It is the study of connections and routes between different points. As a consequence, it is a useful tool for people who route traffic, mail, and electricity. Here is a problem that graph theory would deal with:

Can a highway system be built that connects each of these six points to all the others and yet never crosses itself? If it can, the project would be much less expensive than if a complex interlocking system were necessary.

*A googol is 10^{100}, that is, 1 followed by 100 zeros.

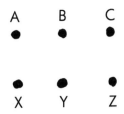

This problem is equivalent to a recreational problem first proposed by Henry Ernest Dudeney in a slightly different form, and is taken from Martin Gardner's collection of his puzzles.

We want to install water, gas, and electricity from W, G, and E to each of the three houses, A, B, and C, without any pipe crossing another. Take your pencil and draw lines showing how this should be done. You will soon find yourself in difficulty.

Solution:

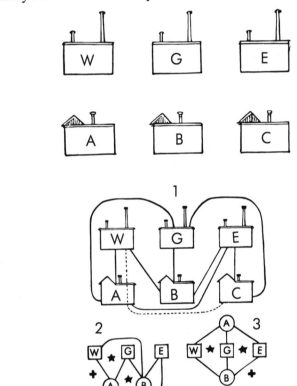

This puzzle can only be solved by a trick. If one householder will allow one pipe for a neighbor to pass through his house, there is no difficulty, and the conditions did not prohibit this not very unreasonable arrangement. Look at figure 1, and you will see that the water pipe for supplying house C passes through house A, but no pipe anywhere crosses another pipe. One is, however, often asked to *prove* that there is no solution without any trick.

Assume that only two houses, A and B, are to be supplied. The relative positions of the various buildings clearly make no difference whatever. Figures 2 and 3 give two positions for the two houses. Wherever you build those houses, the effect will be the same—one of the supply stations will be cut off. In the examples it will be seen that if you build a third house on the outside (say, in the position indicated by one of the black crosses), the gas can never reach you without crossing a pipe. Whereas if you put the house inside one of the enclosures (as indicated by the stars), then you must be cut off either from the water or the electricity—one or the other. But the house must be either inside or outside. Therefore a position is impossible in which it can be supplied from all three stations without one pipe crossing another. Build your two houses wherever you like and you will find that those conditions always obtain.

From Dudeney's problem, it can be seen that there are some connections that are impossible. One way to explore possible and impossible networks is to play around with drawing continuous patterns.

Consider this square:

You can put a pencil down on any point and trace the whole square without picking up your pencil, crossing any line, or going over a line twice. (The illustration shows the tracing line outside the square so you can see it more clearly; actually, you trace right on top of the square.)

Now try to do the same thing with this X:

You'll quickly discover that it is impossible to trace the X in the same way you can trace the square. No matter where you begin, you'll have to go over several lines twice in order to trace the complete shape.

One branch of graph theory studies traceable and nontraceable patterns. However, without going into the complexities of graph theory, it is possible to play with tracing problems and make discoveries about the nature of the traceable. Here are some:

Trace these graphs using one continuous line that does not cross itself (you don't have to end at the same point you began with).

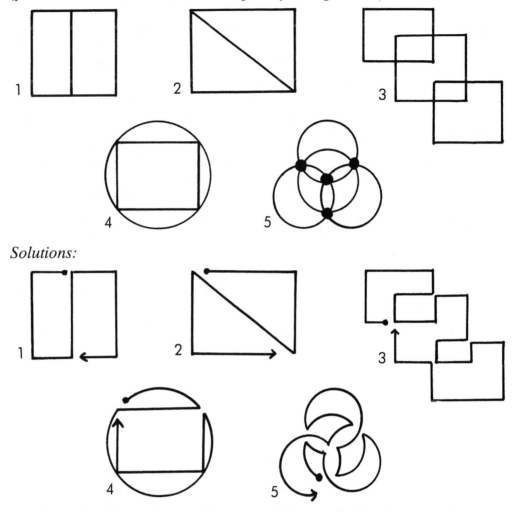

Solutions:

Hint: Graph-tracing problems were first studied by the great German mathematician Leonard Euler, who described a graph by the number of odd and even vertices it had. An even vertex is a meeting point of an even number of lines; an odd vertex is a meeting point of an odd number of lines.

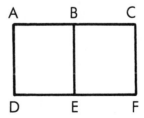

A, C, D, and F are even vertices. B and E are odd vertices.

Euler discovered that you can trace a continuous path and return to

Connections and Tracings

the same point if a graph has only even vertices. Here are some simple examples:

Play with these graphs and see if you can develop a simple strategy for tracing them. Make more even-vertexed graphs.

Euler also discovered that you can trace a graph with a continuous line (though not ending at the same point) if the graph has exactly two odd vertices, as this one does:

All other graphs are not traceable with one continuous line.

To get more insight into the nature of graphs, try to draw a closed graph* with an odd number of odd vertices. If you succeed, please send me your graph as you will have made mathematical history!

an open graph

B

A

C

3 odd vertices

H

G

A   B

F

C   E

D

closing the graph

even: H, D
odd: A, B, C, E,
        F, G

Using the insight of Euler, which of these networks are traceable and which aren't? Convince yourself of that fact by tracing them.

1

2

3

4

5

6

7

8

*A closed graph is one where all line segments are part of a closed geometric shape, such as
□ △ An open graph is the opposite: ⌐ ∧

Solutions:

1. –
2. +
3. –
4. –
5. +
6. +
7. +
8. –

You can make tracing problems for your friends by taking a pattern you know to be traceable and then elaborating on it:

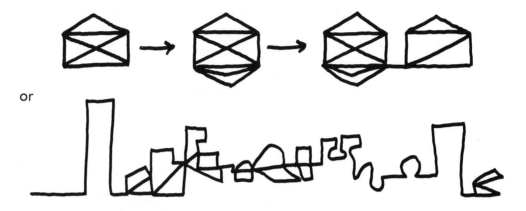

or

Since, from the point of view of drawing networks, curved and straight lines are the same, you can also dress up some simple tracings to make them appear more difficult:

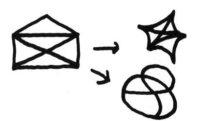

Be sure to save your original tracing and your clues or you may end up with something so elaborate that you have created a puzzle for yourself as well as your friends.

Pattern tracing is quite popular in Zaire, Angola, and Zambia, and children are able to trace in one continuous line patterns that seem impossibly complex. Claudia Zaslavsky has described some of these as follows:

The Chokwe people, who inhabit adjoining regions of Zaire, Angola, and Zambia, have a long tradition of drawing networks in the sand to illustrate their stories. This network poses a riddle. Is the network traceable—can you start at the arrow and trace the figure without taking your pen off the paper, or going over a line more than once? Try to draw your own. First make the dots as a guide.

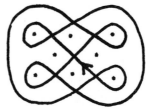

The next beautiful network illustrates the Chokwe people's tale of the beginning of the world. The story tells why the sun and the moon always reappear, but man eventually must die. Start at the arrow, and trace the path to the god Kalunga in one sweep of your pencil. The array of dots serves as a guide when you draw your own network. It is helpful to use graph paper for this one.

The simplest path is to follow each line as far as possible before turning. There are many other paths.

Along the Kasai River in Zaire live the Bakuba people, known widely for the beautiful and intricate patterns in their weaving and wood-carving. Early in the twentieth century, the ethnologist Emil Torday wrote about these people. One day he approached a group of children drawing in the sand. "I was at once asked to peform certain impossible tasks; great was their joy when the white man failed to accomplish them. Draw this design without lifting your finger!"

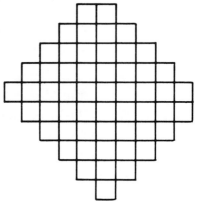

The task is not impossible, but it may be difficult. A good technique is to try some easier problems of the same kind, and build up to the tough one. Here are smaller versions of the network, starting with the most simple. Where do you start; where do you finish? How many small squares in each row or column? What is the growth pattern? Have a few sheets of graph paper handy for experimenting.

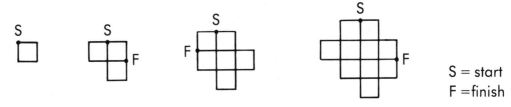

S = start
F = finish

The full network has ten small squares in its longest row or column. Can you draw a larger network of the same shape?

The Bakuba children were imitating the weaving patterns of their elders—the patterns in raffia cloth and in the fishing nets drying on the banks of the river. From the everyday tasks of the village, the Bakuba children had devised a game so sophisticated as to baffle the learned European anthropologist. What better way to learn mathematics!

Here is another Bakuba children's design to trace.

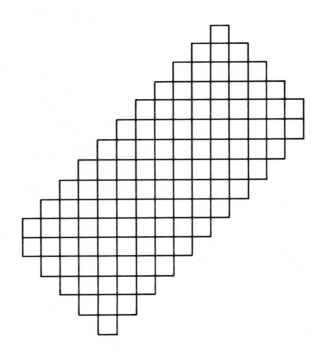

It's interesting that similar patterns come up in Western mathematical recreations. Here are two I discovered:

The Fly's Tour

A fly pitched on the square in the top left-hand corner of a chessboard, and then proceeded to visit every white square. He did this without ever entering a black square or ever passing through the same intersection (where a horizontal and a vertical line meet) more than once. Can you show his route? It can be done in seventeen continuous straight courses.

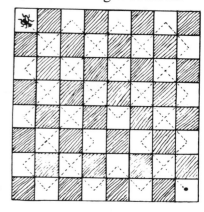

Solution:

The Bishop's Tour

The bishop moves diagonally, and is confined to the squares of a single color. He may move as far as he wishes, in a straight line, at each move.

Find the bishop's tour so that he touches every white square on the board once and only once.

Solution:

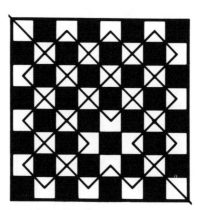

Conway's Connections

John Conway is a mathematician's mathematician and a gamester's gamester. He is well known for his invention of the game Life. Less known is the book *Winning Ways for Your Mathematical Plays,* which he wrote with Elwyn R. Berlekamp and Richard K. Guy (2 vols.; Orlando, Fla.: Academic Press, 1982). *Winning Ways* is an outrageously funny, extremely inventive compound of new and old games surrounded by mathematical analysis. It can be read as a treatise on what are called Conway numbers (imagine having a type of number named for you!), as a source of new and challenging games, as an essay on gaming strategy and game analysis, and as a journey into a world of puns and puzzles both mathematical and linguistic. Section titles such as "The Tweedledum and Tweedledee Argument," "Hackenbush Hotchpotch," "Bogus Nim-Heaps and the Mex Rule," "Sparse Space Spells Speed," and "Numbers, Nimbers and Numberless Wonders" give a flavor of the writing in the book, though they conceal the complexity of some of the mathematics. I must admit that I've been working my way through *Winning Ways*—browsing, jumping from one volume to another and one game to another—for several years and expect never to read it page by page or understand everything in it. Nevertheless, it provides a wonderful journey through the landscape of games and numbers, and I suggest that, if you aren't frustrated by missing half of what you read, it's worth getting and playing with every once in a while.

Sprouts and Brussels Sprouts

Sprouts begins with a number of points drawn on a piece of paper. Start with a two- or three-point game, since the game is more complex than the simple nature of its opening position would indicate. Martin Gardner's description of the game and of its variant Brussels Sprouts follows on the next several pages. He prefaces it with the quotation "I made sprouts fontaneously," from James Joyce's *Finnegans Wake,* which gives you an idea of its flavor. There is probably no better introduction to network drawing than a few weeks' obsession with this game.

The game begins with *n* spots on a sheet of paper. Even with as few as three spots, Sprouts is more difficult to analyze than tick-tack-toe, so it is best for beginners to play with no more than three or four initial spots. A move consists of drawing a line that joins one spot to another or to itself and then placing a new spot anywhere along the line. These restrictions must be observed:

The line may have any shape but it must not cross itself, cross a previously drawn line, or pass through a previously made spot.

No spot may have more than three lines emanating from it.

Players take turns drawing curves. In normal Sprouts, the winner is the last person able to play. As in Nim and other games of the "take-away" type, the game can also be played in a "misère" form, a French term that applies to a variety of card games in the whist family in which one tries to *avoid* taking tricks. In misère Sprouts, the first person unable to play is the winner.

The typical three-spot normal game shown below was won on the seventh move by the first player. It is easy to see how the game got its name, for its sprouts into fantastic patterns as the game progresses. The most delightful feature is that it is not merely a combinatorial game, as so many connect-the-dots games are, but one that actually exploits the topological properties of the plane. In more technical language, it makes use of the Jordan Curve Theorem, which asserts that simple closed curves divide the plane into outside and inside regions.

One might guess at first that a Sprouts game could keep sprouting forever, but Conway offers a simple proof that it must end in at most $3n - 1$ moves. Each spot has three "lives"—the three lines that may meet at that point. A spot that acquires three lines is called a "dead spot," because no more lines can be drawn to it. A game that begins with n spots has a starting life of $3n$. Each move kills two lives, at the beginning and at the end of the curve, but adds a new spot with a life of one. Each move therefore decreases the total life of the game by one. A game obviously cannot continue when only one life remains, since it requires at least two lives to make a move. Accordingly, no game can last beyond $3n - 1$ moves. It is also easy to show that every game must last at least $2n$ moves. The three-spot game starts with nine lives, must end on or before the eighth move, and must last at least six moves.

The one-spot game is trivial, as the first player has only one possible move: connecting the spot to itself. The second player wins in the normal game (loses in misère) by joining the two spots, either inside or outside the closed curve. These two second moves are equivalent, as far as playing the game is concerned, because before they are made there is nothing to distinguish the inside from the outside of the closed curve. Think of the game as being played on the surface of a sphere. If we puncture the surface by a hole inside a closed curve, we can stretch the surface into a plane so that all points previously outside the curve become inside, and vice versa. This topological equivalence of inside and outside is important to bear in mind, because it greatly simplifies the analysis of games that begin with more than two spots.

Knots, Maps, and
Connections

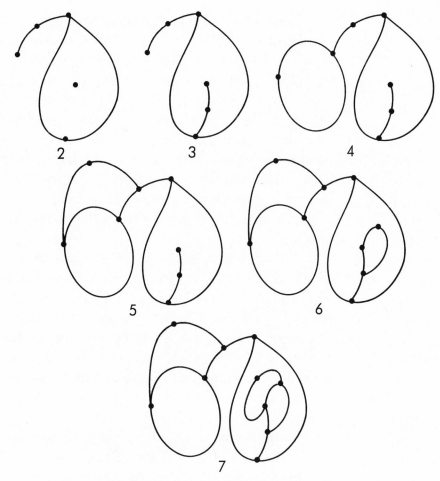

A Typical Game of Three-Spot Sprouts

With two initial spots, Sprouts immediately takes on interest. The first player seems to have a choice of five opening moves, but the second and third openings are equivalent for reasons of symmetry. The same holds true of the fourth and fifth, and, in light of the inside-outside equivalence just explained, all four of these moves can be considered identical. Only two topologically distinct moves, therefore, require exploring. It is not difficult to diagram a complete tree chart of all possible moves, which shows that, in both normal and misère forms of the two-spot game, the second player can always win.

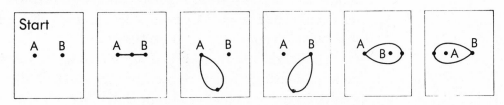

Initial Spots (A and B) and First Player's
Possible Opening Moves in Two-Spot Game

Conway found that the first player can always win the normal three-spot game, and the second player can always win the misère version. Denis P. Mollison, a Cambridge mathematics student, has shown that the first player wins in normal four- and five-spot games. In response to a bet made with Conway that he could not complete his analysis within a month, Mollison produced a forty-nine–page proof that the second player wins the normal form of the six-spot game. The second player wins the misère four-spot game. No one yet knows who has the win in misère games that start with more than four spots. Work has been done on the normal game with seven and eight spots, but no results have been verified. Nor has anyone written a satisfactory computer program for analyzing Sprouts.

Although no strategy for perfect play has been formulated, one can often see toward the end of a game how to draw closed curves that will divide the plane into regions in such a way as to lead to a win. It is the possibility of this kind of planning that makes Sprouts an intellectual challenge and enables a player to improve his skill at the game. But Sprouts is filled with unexpected growth patterns, and there seems to be no general strategy that one can adopt to make sure of winning. Conway estimates that a complete analysis of the eight-spot game is beyond the reach of present-day computers.

Sprouts was invented on the afternoon of Tuesday, February 21, 1967, when Conway and a graduate student, Michael Stewart Paterson, had finished having tea in the mathematics department's common room and were doodling on paper in an effort to devise a new pencil-and-paper game. Conway had been working on a game invented by Paterson that originally involved the folding of attached stamps, and Paterson had put it into pencil-and-paper form. They were thinking of various ways of modifying the rules when Paterson remarked, "Why not put a new dot on the line?"

"As soon as this rule was adopted," Conway writes, "all the other rules were discarded, the starting position was simplified to just n points, and Sprouts sprouted." The importance of adding the new spot was so great that all parties concerned agree that credit for the game should be on the basis of three-fifths to Paterson and two-fifths to Conway. "And there are complicated rules," Conway adds, "by which we intend to share any monies which might accrue from the game."

The name "Sprouts" was given the game by Conway. An alternative name, "Measles," was proposed by a graduate student because the game is catching and it breaks out in spots, but Sprouts was the name by which it quickly became known. Conway later invented a superficially similar game that he calls "Brussels Sprouts" to suggest that it is a joke.

Brussels Sprouts begins with *n* crosses instead of spots. A move consists of extending any arm of any cross into a curve that ends at the free arm of any other cross or the same cross; then a crossbar is drawn anywhere along the curve to create a new cross. Two arms of the new cross will, of course, be dead, since no arm may be used twice. As in Sprouts, no curve may cross itself or cross a previously drawn curve, nor may it go through a previously made cross. As in Sprouts, the winner of the normal game is the last person to play and the winner of the misère game is the first person who cannot play.

After playing Sprouts, Brussels Sprouts seems at first to be a more complicated and more sophisticated version. Since each move kills two crossarms and adds two live crossarms, presumably a game might never end. Nevertheless, all games do end, and there is a concealed joke that the reader will discover if he succeeds in analyzing the game. To make the rules clear, a typical normal game of two-cross Brussels Sprouts is shown that ends with victory for the second player on the eighth move:

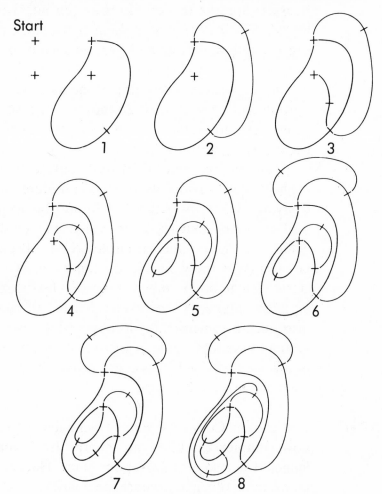

Typical Game of Two-Cross Brussels Sprouts

A letter from Conway reports several important breakthroughs in Sproutology. They involve a concept he calls the "order of moribundity" of a terminal position, and the classification of "zero order" positions into five basic types: louse, beetle, cockroach, earwig, and scorpion. The larger insects and arachnids can be infested with lice, sometimes in nested form, and Conway draws one pattern he says is "merely an inside-out earwig inside an inside-out louse." Certain patterns, he points out, are much lousier than others. And there is the FTOZOM (fundamental theorem of zero-order moribundity), which is quite deep.

Sprouts made an instant hit with *Scientific American* readers, many of whom suggested generalizations and variations of the game. Ralph J. Ryan III proposed replacing each spot with a tiny arrow, extending from one side of the line, and allowing new lines to be drawn only to the arrow's point. Gilbert W. Kessler combined spots and crossbars in a game he called "Succotash." George P. Richardson investigated sprouts on the torus and other surfaces. Eric L. Gans considered a generalization of Brussels Sprouts (called "Belgian Sprouts") in which spots are replaced by "stars"—n crossbars crossing at the same point. Vladimir Ygnetovich suggested the rule that a player, on each turn, has a choice of adding one, two, or no spots to his line.

Several readers questioned the assertion that every game of normal Sprouts must last at least $2n$ moves. They sent what they believed to be counterexamples, but in each case failed to notice that every isolated spot permits two additional moves.

Why is the game of Brussels Sprouts, which appears to be a more sophisticated version of Sprouts, considered a joke by its inventor, John Conway? The answer that it is impossible to play Brussels Sprouts either well or poorly because every game must end in exactly $5n - 2$ moves, where n is the number of initial crosses. If played in standard form (the last to play is the winner), the game is always won by the first player if it starts with an odd number of crosses, by the second player if it starts with an even number. (The reverse is true, of course, in misère play.) After introducing someone to Sprouts, which is a genuine contest, one can switch to the fake game of Brussels Sprouts, make bets, and always know in advance who will win every game. Prove for yourself that each game must end in $5n - 2$ moves.

Hackenbush and Hack

I've chosen Conway's game Hackenbush to use as another example of how complex thinking can emerge from very simple games and challenges. I'm also offering a poor man's Hackenbush, which I call Hack, as an example of a game where the board is created during the course of play and the players have the double role of figuring the most advantageous board to build as well as the best way to play on the resulting board.

Simple Broken Line–Solid Line Hackenbush is described by Conway as an easy paper-and-pencil game "played with a picture." Call the two players left and right. Left moves by erasing any broken line, together with any broken lines that are no longer connected to the ground. Right moves by erasing a solid line in a similar way. Soon, one of the players will find he cannot move because there are no lines of his type in what remains of the picture, and whoever is trapped in this way is the loser.

Here is a simple example of the game:

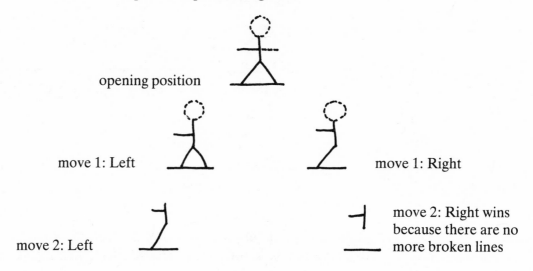

Below are six more Hackenbush beginning situations for games with two players. Decide

- which line to play
- who moves first.

A Point on the Ground

A Foot on the Ground

Two Feet on the Ground

Bridge   Bridge Out   Cantilever

Before analyzing these simple Hackenbush pictures, play with them. All you'll need is a pencil and a piece of paper, though a chalkboard is much more convenient. If you can't find a partner, play both sides yourself. It will give you a sense of the best strategy for a given line and picture.

A Point on the Ground has 2 broken and 2 solid lines. In this game the second player wins, whatever line he or she chooses. If Broken Line goes first, for example, and takes *b*, then Solid Line simply takes *a* and cuts *d* and *c* out of the game. If Broken Line takes *d* as a first move, then Solid Line takes *c*, leaving Broken Line with *b*. The final move is made by Solid Line taking *a*. Here's a visual representation of this strategy:

Broken Line to move first

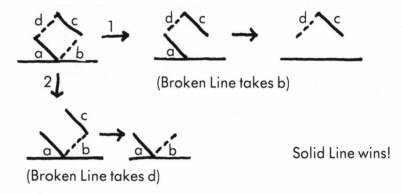

(Broken Line takes b)

(Broken Line takes d)

Solid Line wins!

A Foot on the Ground is a more complex picture but a much simpler game. Having only one foot on the ground when it is Solid Line's turn to move is a guarantee he or she will win. Just take *a*, and the rest of the edifice collapses.

Two Feet on the Ground is a more complex game. There are seven lines, some curved in the form that Conway calls petals or balloons. However, if Broken Line moves first and takes *c*, then everything disappears with the exception of *a* and *g*. Solid Line has to take *a*, and then Broken Line takes *g* and wins. If Solid Line moves first and takes *a*, then Broken Line takes *g* and wins. If Solid Line takes anything else, then Broken Line once again takes *c* and wins after one more move. This situation can be said to be unstable in favor of Broken Line, with *c* being the key element of balance in the outcome of the game.

In Bridge, if Broken Line moves first and takes either *e* or *a*, then he or she has a guaranteed win. Play the game until you convince yourself of this. If Broken Line moves second, a win is also guaranteed.

Play and analyze the last two games yourself.

There is no limit to the number of possible Broken Line–Solid Line Hackenbush situations. Draw some yourself and ask other people to play them. Develop a series of similar challenges of increasing complexity, and play and analyze them. Introduce a third line to make the game a three-player game (using different colors makes the game easily expandable).

And if you want to try a further variant, try Reverse Hackenbush, or what I've called Hack.

Each player (I've only tried a two-person game) chooses a line. Part one of the game is to build a Hackenbush picture. Part two is then to play Hackenbush and see who wins the game played with the constructed picture. I've found that the following minimal rules make the game playable and usually interesting. Of course, you can make up your own rules or vary mine.

Each picture has a set number of lines (or hoops, curves, etcetera), of which each player draws half.

Players can create lines of their own or connect up with each other's line.

There is no limit to the length of any line or to how it curves around the board, so long as it does not cross another line.

Each player has to connect lines with the ground at least once.

There is no limit to the number of times you may connect with the ground. After you've connected one group of lines with the ground, you may draw a nonconnecting line from the ground up or down (what, following Conway's lead, might be called a blade of grass or a root).

Here's an example of a board drawn and a game played with twelve lines, six for each player. This is quite simple. I've found that, the more lines there are, the more interesting and sophisticated the challenges can be.

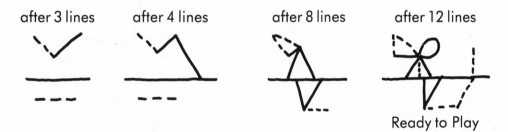

after 3 lines   after 4 lines   after 8 lines   after 12 lines

Ready to Play

What is most interesting to me about this version of Hackenbush is that you have to develop a strategy for playing the game while constructing the board. This means that you have to think ahead all the time, not in the chess way of anticipating moves and exhausting possibilities, but in outthinking your opponent in the very construction of the board to balance the play in your favor.

I couldn't resist including one more example of Conway's connections, this one taken directly from volume 2 of *Winning Ways*. It is Dots and Boxes, a game you might have played when you were a child.

The selection gives a sense of the playful and wild flavor of the book, which is the richest (and perhaps one of the most complex) I know on games and gaming.

Dots and Boxes

> Come, children, let us shut up the box.
> —William Makepeace Thackeray, *Vanity Fair*

> I could never make out what those damned dots meant.
> —Lord Randolph Churchill

Dots and Boxes is a familiar paper-and-pencil game for two players and has other names in various parts of the world. Two players start from a rectangular array of dots and take turns to join two horizontally or vertically adjacent dots. If a player completes the fourth side of a unit square (box), he initials that box and must then draw another line. When all the boxes have been completed, the game ends, and whoever has initialed more boxes is declared the winner.

A player who *can* complete a box is not obliged to do so if he has something else he prefers to do. Play would become significantly simpler were this obligation imposed.

Figure 1 shows Arthur's and Bertha's first game, in which Arthur started. Nothing was given away in the fairly typical opening until Arthur was forced to make the unlucky thirteenth move, releasing two boxes for Bertha. Her last bonus move enabled Arthur to take the bottom three boxes, but he then had to surrender the last four.

This is how most children play, but Bertha is brighter than most. She started the return match with the opening that Arthur had used. He was happy to copy Bertha's replies from that game and was delighted to see her follow it even as far as that unlucky thirteenth move, which had proved his undoing (fig. 2). He grabbed those two boxes and happily surrendered the bottom three, expecting four in return. But Bertha astounded him by giving him back two. He pounced on these but, when he came to make his bonus move, realized he was double-crossed!

Arthur's Move   Bertha's Move   Arthur's Move   Bertha's Move

1   2   3   4

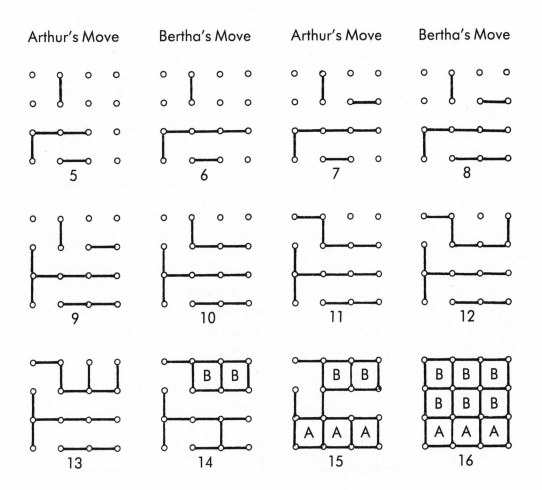

Arthur's Move	Bertha's Move	Arthur's Move	Bertha's Move
5	6	7	8
9	10	11	12
13	14	15	16

1. Arthur's and Bertha's First Game

Bertha beats all her friends in this double-dealing way. Most children play at random unless they've looked quite hard and found that every move opens up some chain of boxes. Then they give the shortest chain away and get back the next shortest in return, and so on.

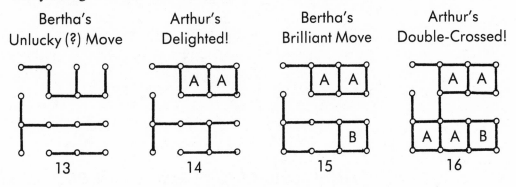

Bertha's Unlucky (?) Move	Arthur's Delighted!	Bertha's Brilliant Move	Arthur's Double-Crossed!
13	14	15	16

2. Bertha's Brilliance Astounds Arthur

But when you open a long chain for Bertha, she may close it off with a double-dealing move that gives you the last two boxes but forces you to open the next chain for her (fig. 3). In this way *she* keeps control right to the end of the game.

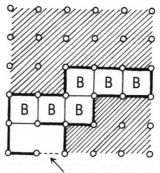

3. Bertha's Double-Dealing Move

You can see in figure 4 just how effective this strategy can be. By politely rejecting two cakes on every plate but the last you offer her, Bertha helps herself to a resounding nineteen to six victory. In the same position, you'd have defeated the ordinary child fourteen to eleven.

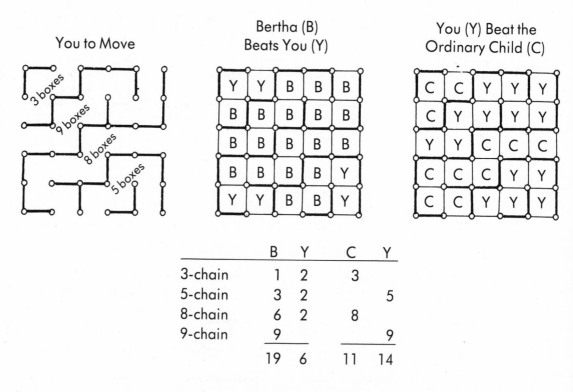

You to Move	Bertha (B) Beats You (Y)	You (Y) Beat the Ordinary Child (C)

	B	Y	C	Y
3-chain	1	2	3	
5-chain	3	2		5
8-chain	6	2	8	
9-chain	9			9
	19	6	11	14

4. Double-Dealing Pays Off!

DOUBLE-DEALING LEADS TO DOUBLE CROSSES
Each double-dealing move is followed, usually immediately, by a move in which two boxes are completed with a single stroke of the pen (fig. 5). These moves are very important in the theory. We'll call them *double-crossed* moves, because whoever makes them usually has been!

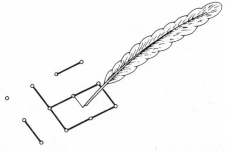

5. A Double-Cross—Two Boxes at a Single Stroke

Now Bertha's strategy suggests the following policy:

> Make sure there are long chains around and try to
> force your opponent to be the first to open one.

Try to Get Control . . .

We'll say that whoever can force his or her opponent to open a long chain has *control* of the game. Then:

> When you have control, make sure you keep it by politely
> declining two boxes of every long chain except the last.

. . . And Then Keep It.

The player who has control usually wins decisively when there are several long chains.

So the fight is really about control. How can you make sure of acquiring this valuable commodity? It depends on whether you're playing the odd- or even-numbered turns. . . .

6. Which Is Dodie and Which Is Evie?

Arthur and Bertha live next to the Parr family, in which there are two sisters called Dodie and Evie (Bertha often teases them by calling them the Parrotty Girls!). You can see them playing the four-box game in figure 6. Dodie's a year younger than Evie and so always has first turn in any game they play. They've got so used to playing like this that even when they're playing somebody else, Dodie always insists on taking the odd-numbered moves while Evie will only take the even-numbered ones:

> Dodie Parr: odd parity
> Evie Parr: even parity

The rule that helps them take control is:

> *Dodie* tries to make the number of
> initial dots + double-crossed moves *odd*.
> *Evie* tries to make this number *even*.

Be *self*ish about Dots + Double Crosses!

In simple games, the number of double crosses will be one less than the number of long chains and this rule becomes:

THE LONG CHAIN RULE

> Try to make the number of
> initial dots + eventual long chains
> *even* if your opponent is *Evie,*
> *odd* if your opponent is *Dodie.*

The *oppo*site for Dots + Long Chains!

The reason for these rules is that, whatever shape board you have on your paper, you'll find that:

$$\begin{array}{l} \text{Number of dots you start with} \\ \underline{+ \text{ Number of double crosses}} \\ = \text{Total number of turns in the game} \end{array}$$

HOW LONG IS "LONG"?

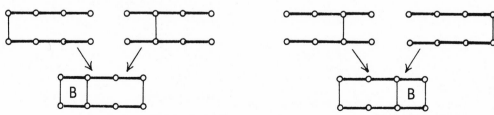

7. Bertha's Endgame Technique

We can find the proper definition of long by thinking about Bertha's endgame technique. A *long chain* is one which contains three or more squares. This is because whichever edge Arthur draws in such a chain, Bertha can take all but two of the boxes in it, and complete her turn by drawing an edge that does not complete a box. Figure 7 shows this for the three-square chain. A chain of two squares is *short* because our opponent might insert the *middle* edge, leaving us with no way of finishing our turn in the same chain. This is called (fig. 8a) the *hard-hearted handout*.

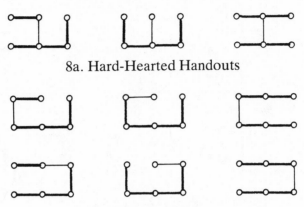

8a. Hard-Hearted Handouts

8b. Half-Hearted Handouts

When you think you are winning, but are forced to give away a pair of boxes, you should always make a hard-hearted handout, so that your opponent has no option but to accept. If you use a *half-hearted* one (fig. 8b), he might reply with a double-dealing move and regain control. But if you're losing, you might try a half-hearted handout. Officially this is a bad move, since your opponent, if he has any sense, will grab both squares. But boys by billions, being bemused by Bertha's brilliance, blindly blunder both boxes back.

THE FOUR-BOX GAME
When Dodie was *very* young, the girls often played the four-box game and offset Dodie's first move advantage by calling it a win for Evie (the second player) when they each got two boxes:

> TWO TWO'S IS A WIN TO TWO

At first Dodie would never give away a box if she could see something else to do, and Evie, who you can see is a very symmetrical player, would always win by copying Dodie's moves on the opposite side of the board. But after watching Bertha playing Evie, Dodie found how to counter this strategy by making a Greek gift on her seventh move. Evie can still win if

Dodie dares to stray from the Path of Righteousness but must resist her temptation to make *every* move a symmetrical one (fig. 9).

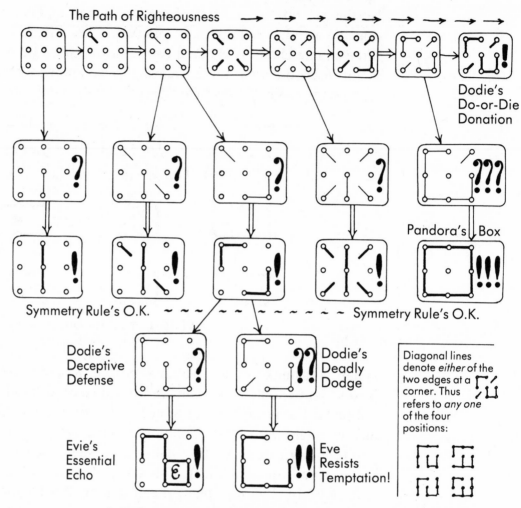

9. Evie Envisaging Every Eventuality

Even though Dodie has the win, it's much harder to write out in full her best plays against sufficiently cunning opponents. This little game is full of traps for the unwary, and those of you who want to become Professional Boxers will find these tables very useful in the bruising preliminary contests on the four-box board.

If the chain lengths are

4		loop of 4
	or	2 + 2
3 + 1		1 + 1 + 1 + 1

the winner will usually be

Dodie	or	Evie

in agreement with the Long Chain Rule. But on this small board, Dodie should often defy the rule and win by splitting the chains as 2 + 1 + 1.

THE NINE-BOX GAME

Surprisingly, the Long Chain Rule makes the nine-box game seem easier than the four-box one. This time Evie wins, and her basic strategy is to draw four spokes as in figure 10, forcing every long chain to go through the center. Against most children this wins for Evie by at least six to three, but Dodie can hold her down to five to four, perhaps by sacrificing the center square, after which Evie should abandon her spoke strategy. Of course, Evie's real aim is to arrange that there's just one long chain, and she often improves her score by forming this chain in some other way.

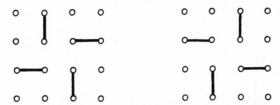

10. Lucky Charms Ward Off More Than One Long Chain;
Evie Puts Spokes in Dodie's Wheel

Evie usually prefers to put her spokes in squares where another side is already drawn, and she's careful to draw spokes in only *one* of the two patterns of figure 10. There usually aren't any double-crossed moves, so that Evie wins at the (16 + 0 =) sixteenth turn.

Dodie tries to arrange *her* moves so that some spoke can only be inserted as a sacrifice, and *either* cuts up the chains as much as possible (maybe with a center sacrifice) *or* forms *two* long chains when Evie isn't thinking. Every now and then a half-hearted handout has saved the game for her just when she thought that all was lost.

Logic and Strategy

The Puzzling Dr. Smullyan

Logic Puzzles

Following Directions

Some Crossings

New Tic-Tac-Toe

Take a Dot or Two

Chessboard Challenges

Some Games from Martin's Garden

Give me a clear blue sky over my head, and the green turf beneath my feet, a winding road before me, and a three hours' march to dinner—and then to thinking! It is hard if I cannot start some games on these lone heaths.
—William Hazlitt, *Tabletalk,* "On Going on a Journey"

The Puzzling Dr. Smullyan

"Contrariwise," continued Tweedledee, "if it was so, it might be; and if it were so, it would be; but as it isn't, it ain't. That's logic."
—Lewis Carroll, *Through the Looking Glass*

Logical thought is full of "ifs," "thens," "ors," "ands," and "nots." However, these deceptively simple words can be combined in ways that lead to complex and sophisticated reasoning. Consider this sentence:

This sentence is not true.

Is it true? Well, if it is true, then it is not true. If it is not true, then it is true. This paradox results from the fact that the sentence is talking about itself. It is one of the quirks of *not* in self-referring sentences.

The master of self-referring paradoxes is Raymond Smullyan, professor of mathematics and philosophy at the City University of New York and author of *What Is the Name of This Book?: The Riddle of Dracula and Other Logical Puzzles* (Englewood Cliffs, N.J.: Prentice-Hall, 1978). Here is a simple Smullyan puzzle followed by more sophisticated challenges. Once one gets a taste of Smullyan's work and the elegance of his presentation of logical problems, it is difficult not to follow him on all his fantastical logical journeys.

The Politician

A certain convention numbered 100 politicians.

Each politician was either crooked or honest. We are given the following two facts:

• At least one of the politicians was honest.
• Given any two of the politicians, at least one of the two was crooked.

Can it be determined from these two facts how many of the politicians were honest and how many of them were crooked?

Solution:

A fairly common answer is "50 honest and 50 crooked." Another rather frequent one is "51 honest and 49 crooked." Both answers are wrong. Now let us see how to find the correct solution.

We are given the information that at least one person is honest. Let us pick out any one honest person, whose name, say, is Frank. Now pick any of the remaining 99; call him John. By the second given condition, at least one of the two men—Frank, John—is crooked. Since Frank is not crooked, it must be John. Since John arbitrarily represents any of the remaining 99 men, then each of those 99 men must be crooked. So the answer is that one is honest and 99 are crooked.

Another way of proving it is this: the statement that given any two, at least one is crooked, says nothing more or less than given any two, they are not both honest; in other words, no two are honest. This means that at most one is honest. Also (by the first condition), at least one is honest. Hence exactly one is honest.

Bellini or Cellini?

Whenever Bellini fashioned a casket he always wrote a true inscription on it, and whenever Cellini fashioned a casket, he always wrote a false inscription on it. Now, Bellini and Cellini had sons who were also casket makers. The sons took after their fathers; any son of Bellini wrote only true statements on those caskets he fashioned, and any son of Cellini wrote only false statements on his caskets.

Let it be understood that the Bellini and Cellini families were the only casket makers of Renaissance Italy. All caskets were made either by Bellini, Cellini, a son of Bellini, or a son of Cellini.

If you should ever come across any of these caskets, they are quite valuable—especially those made by Bellini or Cellini.

1. I once came across a casket that bore the following inscription:

THIS CASKET
WAS NOT MADE
BY ANY SON OF
BELLINI

Who made this casket, Bellini, Cellini, a son of Bellini, or a son of Cellini?

2. Another time I came across a casket whose inscription enabled me to deduce that the casket must have been made by Cellini.
Can you figure out what the inscription could have been?

3. The most valuable caskets of all are those bearing an inscription such that one can deduce that the casket must have been made by Bellini or Cellini, but one cannot deduce which one. I once had the good fortune to come across such a casket. Can you figure out what the inscription could have been?

4. Suppose you came across a casket bearing the following inscription:

THIS CASKET
WAS MADE
BY ME

What would you conclude?

5. A certain Florentine nobleman gave very lavish entertainments, whose high point was a game in which the prize was a valuable jewel. This nobleman knew the story of Portia's caskets from Shakespeare's *Merchant of Venice* and designed his game accordingly. He had three caskets—gold, silver, and lead—and inside one of them was the jewel. He explained to the company that each of the caskets was made by Bellini or Cellini (and not any of their sons). The first person who could guess which casket contained the jewel, and who could prove his guess correct, would be awarded the jewel. Here are the inscriptions:

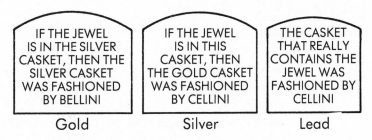

| Gold | Silver | Lead |

Which casket contains the jewel?

Solutions:

1. It was made by Bellini. If a son of Bellini had made the casket, the statement would be false, which is impossible. If Cellini or a son of Cellini had made the casket, the statement would be true, which is impossible. Therefore it was made by Bellini.

2. One inscription that would work is: "This casket was made by a son of Cellini."

3. "This casket was made by Bellini or a son of Cellini."

4. The statement is obviously true, hence the casket was made by Bellini or a son of Bellini.

5. *Step One:* Suppose the lead casket was made by Bellini. Then the statement on it is true, hence the jewel lies in a Cellini casket, so it cannot be in the lead casket. On the other hand, suppose the lead casket was made by Cellini. Then the statement on it is false, hence the jewel lies in a Bellini casket, hence is again not in the lead casket. This proves that the jewel does not lie in the lead casket.

Step Two: Next we know that the jewel cannot lie in the silver casket. If it did, we would get the following contradiction:

Suppose the jewel is in the silver casket. First, suppose the gold casket was made by Bellini. Then the statement on it is true, and since the jewel does lie in the silver casket (by assumption), then the silver casket is a Bellini. From this would follow that the gold casket was made by Cellini. So if the gold is a Bellini, then it is a Cellini.

Step Three: On the other hand, suppose the gold casket is a Cellini.

Then the statement on the gold casket is false, from which follows that the silver casket is not a Bellini, hence is a Cellini. Therefore the statement on the silver casket is false, from which follows that the gold casket is a Bellini. So if the gold casket is a Cellini, then it is a Bellini, which is impossible.

This proves that the jewel cannot be in the silver casket. Therefore it is in the gold casket.

Logic Puzzles

When Flaubert was a very young man, he wrote a letter to his sister, Carolyn, in which he said: "Since you are now studying geometry and trigonometry, I will give you a problem. A ship sails the ocean. It left Boston with a cargo of wool. It grosses 200 tons. It is bound for Le Havre. The mainmast is broken, the cabin boy is on deck, there are 12 passengers aboard, the wind is blowing east-northeast, the clock points to a quarter past three in the afternoon. It is the month of May—How old is the captain?" Flaubert was not only teasing, he was uttering a complaint shared by that large and respectable company "not good at puzzles," that the average puzzle both confuses and overwhelms with superfluous words.

—James Newman, *The World of Mathematics*

Logic puzzles are ones that *give you all the information necessary to solve them.* However, they are usually constructed so that you have to organize the information in ingenious ways in order to achieve the solution. Here's a simple example:

Find a three-letter word such that:
    LEG has no common letter with it.
    ERG has one common letter but not at the correct place.
    SIR has one common letter at the correct place.
    SIC has one common letter, not at the correct place.
    AIM has one common letter, not at the correct place.
One way to go about solving the problem is to begin by making a list of all the words:

LEG

ERG

SIR

SIC

AIM

and, following the statement of the problem, cross out prohibited letters.

LEG has no letter in common with the target word, so the list becomes:

L̶E̶G̶
—R—
SIR
SIC
AIM

ERG has one letter in common but not at the right place, so the word has to have the form R—— or ——R

SIR has one letter in common at the right place, so we now know that the word has the form ——R and that S and I are not in the word. This reduces the list to:

——C
A—M

SIC has one common letter not at the right place. That letter has to be a C, so the word must have the form C—R or —CR. At this stage one would guess that the answer is CAR, but let's check to be sure.

A—M has one common letter. A works, as we've seen, and M would lead to CMR or MCR, neither of which is a word. Thus the guess is right.

Here's another logic problem that is easier to solve than it might first seem:

Find a four-letter word, knowing that each of the following words have two letters in common with it which are not in the correct places:

EGIS
PLUG
LOAM
ANEW

Answer: Gale.

Strategy: the eight letters of EGIS and LOAM are all different; therefore the four letters of the target word are among them. From this one can deduce which four letters make up the word. From there on in, the going is mechanical.

Some of the most interesting logic problems I've seen are dreamed up by Alan Duncum, whose puzzle volumes are regularly published in England. Duncum has provided a wonderful introduction to his puzzles along with help in solving them. You'll notice that they resemble the previous two puzzles, though they are much more elaborate. Here is his introduction, along with four of his puzzles.

How to Solve Logic Problems

Welcome to the world of Logic Problems! They may *look* complicated, but you don't need any specialist knowledge to solve them. You'll soon find that common sense and a cool head are all that are required to meet the challenge.

With each problem we provide a chart that takes into account every possibility to be considered in the solution. First, carefully read the statement of the problem in the introduction, and then consider the clues. Next, enter in the chart all the information immediately apparent from the clues, using an X to show a definite *no* and a ✔ to show a definite *yes*. You'll find that this narrows down the possibilities and might even reveal some new definite information. So now reread the clues with these new facts in mind to discover further positive/negative relationships.

Be sure to enter information in *all* the relevant places in the chart, and to transfer newly discovered information from one part of the chart to all the other relevant parts. For instance, if you know that *X* is *Y*, and you then discover that *Y* is not *Z*, then you also know that *X* is not *Z*.

The smaller grid at the end of each problem is simply a quick-reference chart for your findings.

Three children live in the same street. From the two clues given below, can you discover each child's full name and age?

Clues:
1. Miss Brown is three years older than Mary.
2. The child whose surname is White is 9 years old.

Solution:
Miss Brown (clue 1) cannot be Brian, so you place an X in the Brian/Brown box. Clue 1 tells us that she is not Mary either, so you can put an X in the Mary/Brown box.

Miss Brown is therefore Anne, the only possibility remaining. Now you place a ✔ in that box in the chart, with corresponding X's against the other possible surnames for Anne.

If Anne Brown is three years older than Mary (clue 1), she must be 10 and Mary 7. So place ✔'s in the Anne/10, Brown/10, and Mary/7 boxes, and X's in all the empty boxes in each row and column containing these ✔'s.

	Brown	Green	White	7	9	10
Anne	✔	X	X	X	X	✔
Brian	X			X		X
Mary	X			✔	X	X
7	X					
9	X					
10	✔	X	X			

The chart now reveals Brian's age as 9, so you can place a ✔ in the Brian/9 box. Clue 2 tells us that White is 9 years old too, so he must be Brian. Place a ✔ in the White/9 box and X's in the remaining empty boxes in that row and column, then place a ✔ in the Brian/White box and X's in all the remaining empty boxes in that row and column.

	Brown	Green	White	7	9	10
Anne	✔	X	X	X	X	✔
Brian	X	X	✔	X	✔	X
Mary	X		X	✔	X	X
7	X		X			
9	X	X	✔			
10	✔	X	X			

You can see now that the remaining unfilled boxes in the chart must contain ✔'s, since their rows and columns contain only X's, so they reveal Green as the surname of 7-year-old Mary.

In summary:
Mary Green, 7.
Brian White, 9.
Anne Brown, 10.

Incidentally, it's worth bearing in mind that, while we've tried to arrange the logic problems in ascending order of difficulty, individual solvers tend to differ in their assessment of what constitutes a hard or easy problem. So don't be too surprised if you find the second or third problem, say, easier than the first—a logic problem is a highly individual affair!

You're nearly ready now to tackle a full-size problem. Before you do that, though, have a go at the smaller problem given below. Look on it as a kind of limbering-up exercise for the more taxing logical gymnastics that follow.

Limbering Up

Three customers were in the Post Office. From the information given below, can you discover their names, and find out what purchase each made and in which order they were served?

Clues:
1. The man who bought the stamps was not served first.
2. The person named Smith bought the postal order.
3. Adam was served immediately before Josephine, whose surname is not Robinson.

4. It was the last customer who bought the television license.*

	Adam	Josephine	Neville	Brown	Robinson	Smith	Postal Order	Stamps	Television license
First									
Second									
Third									
Postal Order									
Stamps									
Television license									
Brown									
Robinson									
Smith									

Order	First Name	Surname	Purchase

Solution:

The last customer bought the television license (clue 4). The man who bought the stamps was not served first (clue 1), so he must have been served second, and the first customer must have bought the postal order. Therefore the first customer's surname must be Smith (clue 2). This cannot be Josephine, who was served after Adam (clue 3), while it was a man who bought the stamps (clue 1), so Josephine must have been served third and bought the television license. We know that her surname is not Smith; nor is it Robinson (clue 3); so it must be Brown. Therefore the second customer must have been Mr. Robinson. Clue 3 tells us that this is Adam, so Mr. Smith, who bought the postal order, must be called Neville.

*In Great Britain and many European countries, you are required to buy a license for your television set every year. The money supports the government-run channels, which do not show any commercials.

In summary:

First, Neville Smith, postal order.

Second, Adam Robinson, stamps.

Third, Josephine Brown, television license.

Soft Options

Five friends made soft toys for the crafts stall at their school bazaar. From the information given below, can you say which lady made each toy and determine its color and price?

Clues:

1. The cheapest toy was the mouse, while the pink one was the most expensive.

2. It was Patty who made the elephant.

3. The yellow toy was more expensive than the green one.

4. The cat was blue; Nora's toy did not cost $3.00.

5. Ruth made the white toy, and Mary's offering was priced at $1.00; neither this toy nor the mouse was green.

6. Denise did not make either the lion or the toy which cost exactly $1.50.

	Cat	Elephant	Lion	Monkey	Mouse	Blue	Green	Pink	White	Yellow	$.50	$1.00	$1.50	$2.00	$3.00
Denise															
Mary															
Nora															
Patty															
Ruth															
$.50															
$1.00															
$1.50															
$2.00															
$3.00															
Blue															
Green															
Pink															
White															
Yellow															

Name	Toy	Color	Price

Solution:

Mary's toy cost $1.00 (clue 5), and the mouse was $.50 (clue 1). As the latter is not green (clue 5), and the yellow toy was more expensive than the green one (clue 3), the yellow toy must have cost at least $1.50 so it could not have been made by Mary. Nor was her toy either the green one (clue 5), or the pink one, which cost $3.00 (clue 1), and Ruth made the white one (clue 5), so Mary's toy must have been blue, and was therefore the cat (clue 4). We now know that the green toy did not cost $.50 or $1.00, and we also know that the pink toy cost $3.00, so, as the green toy cost less than the yellow one, it must have been $1.50, and the yellow one must have cost $2.00. This leaves the $.50 mouse revealed as white, and therefore made by Ruth. Patty made the elephant (clue 2), so, as Denise did not make the lion (clue 6), her toy must have been the monkey, and, by elimination, the lion must have been made by Nora. This did not cost $3.00 (clue 4), nor was its price $1.50 (clue 6), so it must have been priced at $2.00, and was therefore yellow. As Denise did not make the green toy costing $1.50 (clue 6), that must have been Patty's elephant, leaving Denise's monkey as the pink toy priced at $3.00.

In summary:
Denise, monkey, pink, $3.00.
Mary, cat, blue, $1.00.
Nora, lion, yellow, $2.00.
Patty, elephant, green, $1.50.
Ruth, mouse, white, $.50.

Good Companions

During the first week of Wendy's school holidays, she spent each day with a different friend. From the information given below, can you determine which day she spent with each friend, and what they did in the morning and afternoon of each day?

Clues:

1. It rained heavily all day on Friday, so Wendy and her friend had to stay in the house.

2. Wendy and Zoe spent the afternoon horseback riding.

3. Louise, who cannot ride a bicycle, spent Thursday with Wendy. They did not go shopping together.

4. Wendy went swimming with Marianne two days before she spent the afternoon gardening.

5. Karen does not play chess.

6. Wendy did not play tennis either on Tuesday or on the day she went swimming, and she did not go shopping the same day that she worked in the garden.

	Annabel	Karen	Louise	Marianne	Zoe	Morning — Bird Watching	Morning — Cycling	Morning — Chess	Morning — Shopping	Morning — Swimming	Afternoon — Gardening	Afternoon — Riding	Afternoon — Records	Afternoon — Tennis	Afternoon — Walking
Monday															
Tuesday															
Wednesday															
Thursday															
Friday															
Afternoon — Gardening															
Afternoon — Riding															
Afternoon — Records															
Afternoon — Tennis															
Afternoon — Walking															
Morning — Bird watching															
Morning — Cycling															
Morning — Chess															
Morning — Shopping															
Morning — Swimming															

Day	Companion	Morning activity	Afternoon activity

Solution:

Since Wendy stayed in the house all day on Friday (clue 1), she must have spent the morning playing chess and the afternoon listening to records. Her companion that day was not Karen, who does not play chess (clue 5); Zoe, who went horseback riding with her (clue 2); Louise, who was her Thursday companion (clue 3); or Marianne, who went swimming (clue 4). So she must have been Annabel. Wendy did not go swimming with Marianne on Thursday or Friday (clue 4), nor on Tuesday (clue 6), so that activity must have taken place on either Monday or Wednesday. Had it been Wednesday, she would have spent Friday afternoon gardening (clue 4), which we know she did not, so she must have gone swimming on Monday morning, and therefore gardened on Wednesday afternoon. We know that Zoe spent her afternoon with Wendy horseback riding, and that Louise was her Thursday companion, so the girl who helped her in the garden on Wednesday must have been Karen. By elimination, Zoe must have spent Tuesday with Wendy. Wendy did not play tennis on the day she went swimming, Monday (clue 6), so she must have played tennis with Louise on Thursday afternoon, and, by elimination, she must have gone for a walk on Monday afternoon with Marianne. Clue 3 tells us that Wendy and Louise did not go cycling or shopping on Thursday morning, so they must have spent the time bird watching. Nor did Wendy go shopping on the day she worked in the garden, Wednesday (clue 6), so she must have gone shopping with Zoe on Tuesday, and spent Wednesday morning cycling with Karen.

In summary:
   Monday, Marianne, swimming, walking.
   Tuesday, Zoe, shopping, horseback riding.
   Wednesday, Karen, cycling, gardening.
   Thursday, Louise, bird watching, tennis.
   Friday, Annabel, playing chess, listening to records.

An interesting exercise is to draw your own logical grid and work backward from an answer to a problem of your own. One simple way is to take a problem given here and substitute different numbers, names, and categories. Once you have created a problem of your own using simple substitution, it becomes easier to vary the problem and invent one that is quite different than the sample.

Following Directions

I never thought that following directions could be fun. In fact, I have the perverse habit of trying to solve problems by defying or ignoring the directions. However, recently I discovered a book by Anita Harnadek called *Following Directions—B,* which is part of a wonderful thinking-skills curriculum published by Midwest Publications. The book is full of instructions on how to draw and write on a piece of blank paper. The instructions use principles of logic in a clever and delightful way. Before looking at examples from the book, try this little one I made up:

Directions:

1. If it is a sunny day, draw a star in the upper right corner of your piece of paper.

2. If it is not a sunny day, skip to direction 4.

3. Draw someone watching the star.

4. Draw a quarter-moon in the lower left corner of the paper.

5. If you were born in an odd-numbered month of the year, draw a spiral that radiates out two inches from the center of the paper.

6. If you were born in an even month of the year, add up all of the digits of the year you were born in and write the sum in the middle of the paper.

7. If your age is a prime number, tear up your paper and take a walk.

8. If your age is a square or cube, turn the paper 180 degrees and start again at direction 1.

9. If your age is any other number, turn the paper over and start again at direction 1.

Here are some of the exercises from the book. Make up your own and go crazy with logic.

Directions:

1. Write your name in the upper right corner of your paper.

2. You are going to make three dots somewhere around the middle of your paper. You must make them so that a straight line cannot be drawn through all of them at once. And you must make them so that no two of the dots are closer to each other than about one inch. Make the three dots now.

3. Draw segments so that each pair of dots is connected.

4. Just below your name, write the number of segments you have so far.

5. Make another dot anywhere on your paper, except that it cannot

fall in a place where a single straight line can connect it with both of two other dots.

6. Draw segments connecting your latest dot to all the other dots.

7. Just below the last number you wrote, write the number of segments you have so far.

8. Repeat directions 5 through 7 twice.

Directions:

1. Write your name at the upper right corner of your paper.

2. In the middle of your paper, draw a large square so that one side is facing the bottom of the paper.

3. In the order named, make a dot in the center of the top of the square, in the center of the left side of the square, in the center of the bottom of the square, and in the center of the right side of the square.

4. In the order named, draw segments connecting the first and the second dots, the second and third dots, the third and fourth dots, and the fourth and first dots.

5. In the same order you drew the segments, make a dot in the center of each segment you just drew.

6. In the order mentioned, draw segments connecting the fifth and sixth dots, the sixth and seventh dots, the seventh and eighth dots, and the eighth and fifth dots.

7. Thinking of the segments you made for direction 6 above, draw segments ending at the centers of the first and second segments, the second and third segments, the third and fourth segments, and the fourth and first segments.

8. Count the number of triangles on your paper. Write this number to the left of your name.

9. Count the number of squares on your paper. Write this number under your answer to direction 8 above.

10. Just under the last number you wrote, write the product of the two numbers you wrote.

11. Add all the numbers you wrote. If the sum is more than 70, write the sum between your first and last names. If the sum is 70, write the sum just under the last number you wrote. If the sum is less than 70, write the sum in the center of the last square you drew.

Finally, Sonja Prioleau of John's Island, South Carolina, offers this nifty "test" she recalls from her schooldays. It's a fine one for teachers to give.

Directions:

1. Read all directions thoroughly before proceeding.

2. Print your name, class, and the date in the upper right corner of your test paper. Then work the following problems.

3. The Jones family pays $30 more than one-third of its total monthly income for rent. If the family's rent is $370 a month, how much is its total monthly income?

4. Add 3.5, .049, .07, and 2.

5. A cake mold has a diameter of 9 inches. It is 4 inches deep. To avoid spills, we want to fill it only three-quarters full of batter. How much batter (in cubic inches) will we need?

6. Recheck all your answers.

7. If you have followed direction 1 exactly, ignore directions 2 through 6. Just sign your name on your test paper and you'll get an A.

Some Crossings

Perhaps the most famous crossing problem is: "Why did the chicken cross the road?" The answer, "To get to the other side," could be mathematically interesting if we drew the road on a Möbius strip or made it into a maze or placed it within a non-Euclidean space. However, one doesn't have to twist a simple bad joke into a crossing problem, because there are many traditional problems that provide interesting logical challenges. Versions of these problems can be found in cultures throughout the world, and some are thousands of years old. Here is one that comes from Charlemagne's time (late ninth and early tenth centuries):

A traveler comes to a riverbank with his possessions: a wolf, a goat, and a head of cabbage. The only available boat is very small and can carry no more than the traveler and *one* of his possessions. Unfortunately, if left together, the goat will eat the cabbage and the wolf dine on the goat. How can the traveler transport his belongings to the other side of the river, keeping his vegetable and animals intact?

Here are two solutions:

| W = Wolf | C = Cabbage | G = Goat | → = Crossing |
Trip	On One Shore	In Boat	On Opposite Shore
1	W, C	G→	
2	W, C	←	G
3	C	W→	G
4	C	←G	W
5	G	C→	W
6	G	←	W, C
7		G→	W, C

Trip	On One Shore	In Boat	On Opposite Shore
W = Wolf	C = Cabbage	G = Goat	→ = Crossing
1	W, C	G→	
2	W, C	←	G
3	W	C→	G
4	W	←G	C
5	G	W→	C
6	G	←	C, W
7		G→	C, W

Some more complicated versions of this crossing problem are common in different parts of Africa. Claudia Zaslavsky passes along several river-crossing riddles told by the Kamba people of Kenya (John N. Maundu: UNESCO paper, 1974).

One riddle tells us something of family relations. A man, his wife, and their four parents must cross the river by a boat that can carry a maximum of two people at a time. Due to cultural respect, the man cannot share the boat with either his mother or his wife's parents. And the woman cannot share the boat with her father or her husband's parents. All six people can row. How many trips are needed to get everyone across? We might add the condition that no person rows more than twice.

Solution:

W = Wife   Mw = Mother of Wife   Mh = Mother of Husband
H = Husband   Fw = Father of Wife   Fh = Father of Husband

Trip	On One Shore	In Boat	On Opposite Shore
1	Fw, H, Mh, Fh	W, Mw→	
2	Fw, H, Mh, Fh	←Mw	W
3	Fw, H, Fh	Mw, Mh→	W
4	Fw, H, Fh	←Mh	W, Mw
5	H, Fh	Mh, Fw→	W, Mw
6	H, Fh	←Fw	W, Mw, Mh
7	H	Fw, Fh→	W, Mw, Mh
8	H	←Fh	W, Mw, Mh, Fw
9		Fh, H→	W, Mw, Mh, Fw

Another riddle is an invitation to Women's Lib! Three men have recently married, and go to market with their wives. They must cross a stream in a boat that can carry only two people at a time. But no man will leave his wife with another man, either in the boat or on the shore. Again, all six people can row. Find the minimum number of trips necessary.

Solution:

Trip	On One Shore	In Boat	On Opposite Shore
1	W_2, H_2, W_3, H_3	$W_1, H_1 \rightarrow$	
2	W_2, H_2, W_3, H_3	$\leftarrow H_1$	W_1
3	H_1, W_3, H_3	$W_2, H_2 \rightarrow$	W_1
4	H_1, W_3, H_3	$\leftarrow H_2$	W_1, W_2
5	W_3, H_3	$H_1, H_2 \rightarrow$	W_1, W_2
6	W_3, H_3	$\leftarrow W_1, H_1$	H_2, W_2
7	W_1, W_3	$H_1, H_3 \rightarrow$	H_2, W_2
8	W_1, W_3	$\leftarrow H_3$	H_1, H_2, W_2
9	W_1	$W_3, H_3 \rightarrow$	H_1, H_2, W_2
10	W_1	$\leftarrow H_1$	H_2, W_2, H_3, W_3
11		$W_1, H_1 \rightarrow$	H_2, W_2, H_3, W_3

Ms. Zaslavsky offers this bonus:

Now let us travel one-third of the way around the world and over two centuries backward in time to the American colonies. Recently, I acquired a copy of Wingate's *A Treatise of Common Arithmetic*. In the chapter on sports and pastimes are two river-crossing riddles. One is the old familiar problem of the countryman who had to transport a fox, a goose, and a peck of corn. The cast of characters has changed, but not the solution.

The second riddle was a real surprise. Here it is verbatim. "Three jealous husbands with their wives, being ready to pass by night over a river, do find at the river side a boat which can carry but two persons at once, and for want of a waterman they are necessitated to row themselves over the river at several times. The question is, how those six persons shall pass 2 by 2, so that none of the 3 wives may be found in the company of 1 or of 2 men, unless her husband be present?" Cultures are not so different, after all!

New Tic-Tac-Toe

Bernie De Koven is a master gamester and game maker. He has worked with the New Games Foundation, run the Games Preserve in Pennsylvania, and developed computer games for the Children's Computer Workshop. It is impossible to spend time with Bernie without coming away with new perceptions on how old game forms can be modified, or how simple ideas can be turned into sophisticated games. In the mid-1970's when I edited *Gamesemag,* I asked Bernie to do a pamphlet for us on ways in which Tic-Tac-Toe can itself be an object of play. Bernie produced New Tic-Tac-Toe, which is a lovely essay on what could be called metagaming, that is, making up games about games. Take a pencil and paper, and play with Bernie. Then create your own variations of Tic-Tac-Toe. It's possible that you'll end up with a feel for the adventure of creating games. In addition, you should get a feel for how one small mathematical system— the game of tic-tac-toe—works.

Strategy games are minisystems, and playing with their rules is a form of mathematical activity. Bernie's analyses of tic-tac-toe are as much an excursion into mathematical thinking as an exploration of game development.

If you don't know how to play tic-tac-toe, find a friend. Then draw this:

Draw an X in any open space, like this:

Then it's your friend's turn to draw a O in any other empty space:

Then keep on taking turns until one of you has 3 X's or 3 O's in a row   column   or diagonal

If you do know how to play tic-tac-toe, you might have already found out that

- if you go first, you won't lose
- if you go second, you won't win

so you probably don't play the game very much anymore. You need something more challenging, something that doesn't let you be so sure about who is going to win or lose.

But that doesn't mean you have to learn a whole new game. As fun as it is to learn a new game, it's even more fun to make up your own new game. All you have to do to find it is *change a rule of the old game and see what happens.*

What would happen if we made a different kind of board for tic-tac-toe? The rule used to be that the board had to be exactly 3 squares by 3 squares in shape. How about starting with one that's 4 by 4 instead?

Certainly looks like a board. Let's try playing on it to see if we like it. This is how our first game might look:

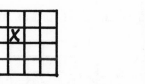

Except that, if you were ○, you would have already lost the game. If you moved then X would move and win.

Or, if you moved then X would move and still win.

The winning strategy in tic-tac-toe is to keep as many ways to make three-in-a-row as you can. Then, if your opponent blocks one way, you can still win the other way.

If we tried the game again, it might look like this:

(○ isn't going to let X use the same trick as before)

But then X plays:

and again, X has two different ways to win, so ○ loses.

It seems that our first try at making a more interesting game didn't work out the way we wanted it to. But we did learn something that should help us find out what we should try next, or what we shouldn't try any more.

In order to have a game that we can have fun with—that's fair and challenging for both players—it's important to know that the winner isn't always the first player. A way to know if we have made up a game that's likely to be fun is: *The second player should have as much chance to win as the first player does.* All this means is that the game should be fair.

If we use the board as we have made it, and if both players know how to play tic-tac-toe, we can be sure that, unless the first player makes a silly mistake, that player will win the game.

Let's try something else.

Our first board was square. It had as many places in its rows as it did in its columns.

4 spaces ↓

4 spaces →

What would happen if we made the board into a rectangle?

Let's try it.

Wait a minute! It looks like X has a sure win again, because if

then O has to block

and X will win.

Before we throw the rectangular board away, let's make sure it really won't work. Let's test it for fairness. Maybe if O tries a different strategy:

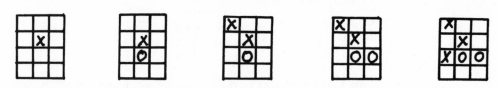

Again, X has two ways to win.

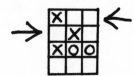

Is there still another strategy for O? If we could find one, the game would be what we want it to be. But it seems that no matter how hard we try, if both players know the game, the first player has a better chance of winning than the second player does.

We might be ready to jump to a conclusion now. The rectangular board is really part of the square board. All we need to do to make the rectangle into a square is to add one more column.

We know that the rectangle doesn't work, so we can also say that if any part of our board is a 3 by 4 rectangle, the first player can always win. That certainly isn't the kind of game we're looking for.

Maybe what we need to do is to change the shape of our board just a little. For example, what would happen if we blocked out one of the spaces in the 3 by 4 rectangle?

Again, we'd better try it before we jump to any conclusions.

It does, in fact, look good, so far. We took away one of X's best moves by blocking that space off, and, when X tried the same trick that worked on the old rectangular board, it didn't help at all.

Let's play it some more. We really might have found what we've been looking for. At least we've got something that's a little more challenging.

Oh, no! It looks like this isn't going to work either. Again, X has two ways to win.

But maybe O didn't use the best strategy. Let's try again.

It's looking a lot better.

Rats! X has two ways to win again.

So, *what would happen if* we blocked off two squares instead of just one. Maybe it will help. After all, if we keep on taking away X's good moves, we should be able to find a fair game sooner or later.

We can do this in many different ways:

This one looks interesting, so let's play with it for a while:

So far, so good. But O has to be a little clever to see the next move.

If O moves to either of the places in the left column, the game will be a tie. Can you see why? Can you see how X might have won if O moved to the middle of the top row?

It does look like this board might really be the one we've been looking for. It all depends on how challenging the game is for you and the people you're playing with.

Now let's experiment with changing other rules of tic-tac-toe.

The Rule: 1. You want to win.

What will happen if the object of the game were to lose instead of win? There is, in fact, a precedent—a rule like that in another game. In the game called Giveaway Checkers, the object is to be the first player to get rid of all of his or her pieces. It turns out that it's just as interesting a game as regular checkers. Now, if we took that idea and tried it with tic-tac-toe, the goal of the game would be to force the other player to win. Will it work? Well, here are some regular tic-tac-toe boards for you to try it on:

\#   \#   \#   \#

Maybe you'll have to change some other rules to make the idea work. It might be worth exploring.

The Rule: 2. A tie is nobody's score.

A tie is usually called a "cat's game." That means that if nobody wins the game, it doesn't count.

What will happen if we were to keep track of all the games we tied and somehow gave those games to the first person to win? How would that work? Let's say that there are two players, Charles and Charlene. They've tied seven games in a row. Then, Charlene wins the next game. So, she gets eight points (seven for the tied games plus one for the game she just won).

As a matter of fact, it turns out that that change isn't really very new. It's an official way of playing tic-tac-toe, only it hasn't been played that way for more than fifty years. I read about it in a book called *The Traditional Games of England, Scotland and Ireland,* by Alice Gomme.* Ms. Gomme describes the game as Noughts (O) and Crosses (X). It was played on a piece of slate (like a little blackboard). The center space on the top of the board was used for scoring ties. These were said to belong to Old Nick or Old Tom. The first player to win after Old Nick got a point would get all of Old Nick's points.

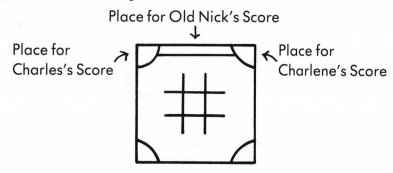

Place for Old Nick's Score

Place for Charles's Score

Place for Charlene's Score

What will happen if the goal of the game is to tie? Now the only score that counts is Old Nick's. As soon as one of us wins, the game is over. The goal of the game would be to see how many points we could get for Old Nick. Old Nick really represents both of us.

This is a fun idea. It would really make the game different. But if you try it, you'll probably find out that you have to change a couple of other rules in order to make this one work.

The Rule: 3. It takes three-in-a-row to win.

What will happen if we change the number it takes to win? We could try four-in-a-row, five-in-a-row—as many as we want.

Naturally, we'll have to change the size of the board, too. To play five-in-a-row, we'll need a board that has at least five spaces in each row and column:

189

New Tic-Tac-Toe

*Reprinted by Dover Books in 1964.

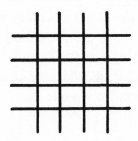

Now, who says that the board has to have exactly five spaces in each row or column? We know that there has to be at least that many spaces, but could the game be played on a board that has more than five spaces? How about a board like this:

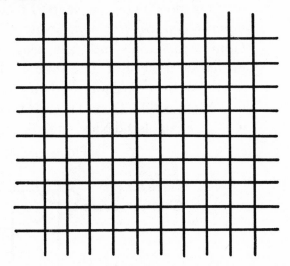

Well, as a matter of fact, once again we've come up with a game that's already been invented. In fact, this game is called Go-Moku and was invented in China thousands of years ago. But the game is new to us, and if we have fun doing it, who cares how new it really is?

Actually, we have to make two other changes in order to have the official game of Go-Moku. First, the board has nineteen lines going each way. Second, another rule is changed:

The Rule: 4. You draw your marks on the empty spaces.

What happens in Go-Moku is that the marks are put at the intersections instead of in the spaces. It doesn't seem to change anything about the way the game is played, but it does, in fact, change a rule.

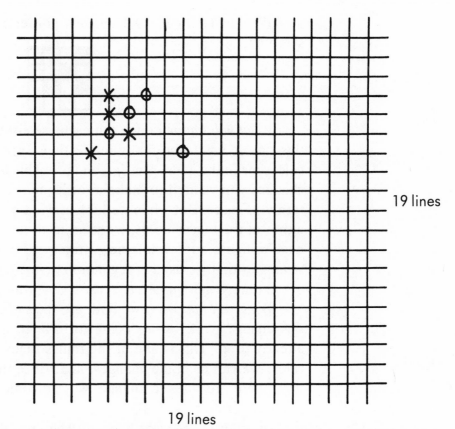

19 lines

19 lines

The Rule: 5. The winning player has his or her marks in a straight line. (This rule is really part of rule 3, which says that the winner has three-in-a-row.)

What will happen if the object of the game is to get three-in-a-triangle, like this:

How about three in a square? Well, that's a little hard to do with just three marks. So, *what will happen if* the object is to get four-in-a-square, or six-in-a-star?

The Rule: 6. One player is X and the other O.
What will happen if we invent new symbols?

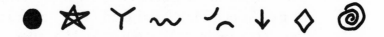

What will happen if we are each a different color instead of a different symbol?

What will happen if we can each use either of the two symbols? Now, this one seems to be really interesting. Inventing new symbols or using colors made the game prettier, and probably led you to discover other rule changes you wanted to make in order to see what happens with the pattern you make. But when we look at what happens when we can each use either of the two symbols, we seem to come up with a game that makes us have to figure out a whole new strategy. If we try to play it using the same strategies that we used in regulation tic-tac-toe, it just doesn't work. Most of the time, *a new game lets us use a new strategy.*

What will happen if we both use the same symbol? (In order to make this change work, we're going to have to use some of the changes we already tried. This is one of the things that make it so exciting to change rules: we can combine changes, and, since there are more combinations than there are rules to change, we can come up with maybe a couple of hundred different games!)

In order to see what happens when we both use the same symbol, we have to try it, or at least imagine what will happen. If we change nothing else about the game, it's clear that whoever goes first will win. That, as we know, means that we haven't come up with an interesting game.

Now, if we play with some of the other changes, such as rules 3, 4, and 5, and mix them up into one game where both players have the same symbols, we might come up with the very famous old game of Dots.

Here's how it might happen: First of all, we notice, from rule 4, that you don't have to draw marks on empty spaces. You can draw them on intersections and have just as good a game. Now, suppose we drew *only* intersections. If we took away the lines and just marked the places where the lines crossed, we'd come up with something that looked like this:

Now, if our mark, instead of an X or O, were changed (according to rule 6) to a straight line, and then, as we explored in rule 5, we tried to get four-in-a-square, look at what would happen:

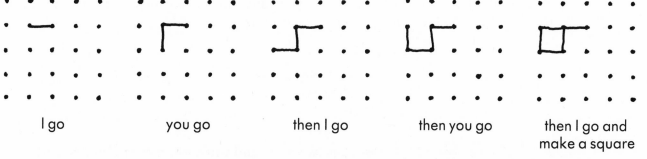

I go   you go   then I go   then you go   then I go and
make a square

The only other rules that we would have to add in order to make our game exactly like Dots are: the player who makes a square puts his or her initial in the square; a square has to be the smallest possible square; if you make a square, you get an extra move; the player with the most squares at the end of the game is the winner.

We went really far away from good old tic-tac-toe when we explored this rule. But, we did come up with a good game, and, in fact, if we started with this game of Dots and played around with some of the rules, we could come up with at least ten more ways of playing with just that one change.

All we have to do is look at the rules and see what would happen if we changed one of them. For example, we could play on a larger or smaller board. We could change the shape of the board (diamond-shaped, round, triangular, maybe even three-dimensional). We could change the shape of the winning pattern (a diamond or a triangle instead of a square). We could change the rule about the extra move (you have to take it, or you don't get it, or you get two extra moves).

Bernie De Koven's play with tic-tac-toe ended up with the transformation of tic-tac-toe into Dots. That transformation is a good example of how mathematical exploration can lead to the discovery of unexpected similarities in superficially different systems. It is also an illustration of how being bold enough to change rules and explore the consequences of those changes can lead to the development of new structures that are at least as interesting as the ones you began with.

Take a Dot or Two

The Take a Dot or Two game is a two-player challenge. You begin with an array of any number of dots, say ten:

o o o o o o o o o o

Then players take turns crossing out one or two dots. The player who takes the last dot wins. Here's a sample game:

Player A takes two	o o o o o o o o
Player B takes one	o o o o o o o
Player A takes two	o o o o o
Player B takes two	o o o
Player A takes one	o o
Player B takes two	and wins, as there are no dots left

This simple game raises a number of questions:

What are the best moves for each player?

Is any player guaranteed a win?

Does it make any difference whether you begin with an even or odd number of dots?

What happens if you can take one, two, or three dots from the array? Does the game get more complex or become boring?

What changes if the player who takes the last dot loses instead of wins?

Does the number of dots in the array make any difference, or can all the arrays be reduced to a simple array?

Is there any general theory where all games of this kind can be described and their solutions (if both players make their best possible moves) predicted?

These are the kinds of questions that mathematical play raises. They are questions about the nature and structure of the game, or what are more formally called metaquestions. Of course one plays the game, but one also thinks about the nature of play, about the structure of the game as well as possible rule changes and strategies. Playing the game is only a small part of playing with the game.

There isn't even any need for a partner in order to play and play with games. One strategy for approaching games is to play sincerely against yourself. In the case of Take a Dot or Two, playing yourself is a good way to get inside of the structure of the game and begin to analyze it. All you have to do is pretend that there are two equally intelligent you's called, for example, U-1 and U-2, and that on each turn you become one of them. Then play with the greatest subtlety and seriousness for both sides.

The habit of playing against oneself is not difficult to develop. As an exercise, take a game you know, such as chess or checkers or tic-tac-toe (some games such as card games with concealed hands don't easily lend themselves to this approach), and play against yourself a few times. I find it a fascinating experience, which gets me to focus more on the feel and play characteristics of the game than playing an opponent does. It also has the virtue of allowing me to play on buses and airplanes and other places where there are no opponents handy.

Sometimes it's useful to approach a game, especially one in which you're playing against yourself, by simplifying it. This helps you get into the rhythm of playful schizophrenia that often leads to insight into game strategy and structure. How about starting, for example, with a very simple version of Take a Dot or Two that uses only three dots (two dots is trivial, with the first move a win):

o   o   o

If U-1 takes one dot, then U-2 takes two dots and wins.

If U-1 takes two dots, then U-2 takes one dot and wins. For the game with three dots, the second player always wins, an immediate and simple mathematical insight—one worth filing away. Now you know that whenever three dots are left in the game, the second player will win, no matter how many dots the game began with.

How about four dots:

o   o   o   o

U-1 takes one dot, leaving a three-dot game, which you already know will be won by the second player to move at that point of the game. No matter what U-2 does, U-1 is guaranteed a win as long as the first move of the game was to take one dot.

This might be a good time to speculate about whether, for any number of dots, one player is guaranteed a win. It might also be worth guessing about what the winning strategy for a particular number of dots is. Your guesses may turn out wrong, but it doesn't make any difference. There's always something to learn while testing them out. Rights and wrongs are much less important in mathematical recreations than participation and exploration.

So far the U's have established that, for a three-dot game, Player 2 is guaranteed to win, and for a two- and a four-dot game, Player 1 is guaranteed a win. How about the hypothesis that odd numbers of dots lead to a guaranteed win for U-2 and an even number of dots to one for U-1?

It's easy to begin to test out that idea. Try five- and six-dot games:

o   o   o   o   o

U-1 takes two, leaving a three-dot game and guaranteeing a win for U-1 because of what we learned before about three-dot games.

o   o   o   o   o   o

Six-dot game:

> U-1 takes two, leaving a four-dot game
>
> U-2 takes one, leaving a three-dot game and therefore winning.
>
> To summarize the results so far:

$$
\begin{array}{cccccc}
 & & & & \circ & \circ \\
 & & & \circ & \circ & \circ \\
 & & \circ & \circ & \circ & \circ \\
 & \circ & \circ & \circ & \circ & \circ \\
\circ & \circ & \circ & \circ & \circ & \circ
\end{array}
\qquad
\begin{array}{l}
\text{U-1} \\
\text{U-2} \\
\text{U-1} \\
\text{U-1} \\
\text{U-2}
\end{array}
$$

Neither the hypothesis about U-1 winning even or odd games nor the hypothesis about U-2 winning odd or even games holds up, as the case of four dots shows. However, by playing with it, some interesting aspects of the dot arrays emerge. One I discovered was that any number that has three as a divisor is an automatic win for U-2. Since fifteen and twelve have three as a divisor, this fact also invalidates the hypothesis of odds and evens.

My discovery was made when playing with the case of six dots and keeping in mind that the player who moves first in a three-dot game always loses. For the six-dot game, U-2 forced U-1 to be the first player in a three-dot game by playing:

$$
\begin{array}{ll}
\text{U-1} & 1 \\
\text{U-2} & \underline{2} \\
 & 3
\end{array}
\qquad
\begin{array}{ll}
\text{U-1} & 2 \\
\text{U-2} & \underline{1} \\
 & 3
\end{array}
$$

I noticed that U-2 was in a position to keep the total score to three, and realized that by doing this for any number of dots evenly divisible by three, the same strategy would work. For example, consider twenty-seven dots:

o o o o o o o o o o o o o o o o o o o o o o o o o o o

and partition them into groups of three's:

o o o/o o o/o o o/o o o/o o o/o o o/o o o/o o o/o o o

By keeping the sum of U-1's and U-2's moves to three, the second player is guaranteed a win.

A final note on play strategy: Whenever your opponent in Take a Dot or Two has to take dots from an array that can be evenly divided by three, you have an automatic win. All you have to do is keep the remaining array divisible by three. Thus, if fifteen dots are left and it is your opponent who is to move, you can guarantee yourself a win by forcing her or him to make moves with: twelve, then nine, then six, then three dots left. The idea is to make every game into the equivalent of a three-dot game with you moving second.

As a challenge, you might want to explore another version—Take a Dot or Two or Three—which allows each player to take one, two, or three dots on a turn. See what you can discover about the nature of the game. Is it interesting, are there obvious strategies for winning, etcetera?

Here are a few specific questions to consider when you explore the game:

- In a four-dot game, which player has a guaranteed win?
- In a five-dot game, which player has a guaranteed win?
- In a six-dot game, which player has a forced win?

Set up a way to demonstrate your answers to other people.

Chessboard Challenges

A number of games are both easy to play and interesting to analyze. Here's a very simple one that is played on a 3-by-3 board, using three black and three white chess pawns placed opposite each other on the board. Play the game a few times. If you can't find another person to play against, take both parts yourself. While you're playing, think about what the best strategy of play is for each player.

The pieces move as in chess—one square forward at a time, with capture on the diagonal only. Therefore, when two pawns are face to face, neither can move unless they can capture diagonally. In the following diagram, the black pawn can capture diagonally to the left or right but cannot capture straight ahead:

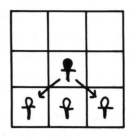

This results in either of the following positions:

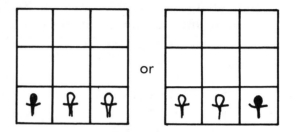

The winner of the game is either the first player to get a pawn to the opposite end of the board or the last person to move. Thus, in the following situations with Black to move, a win is achieved:

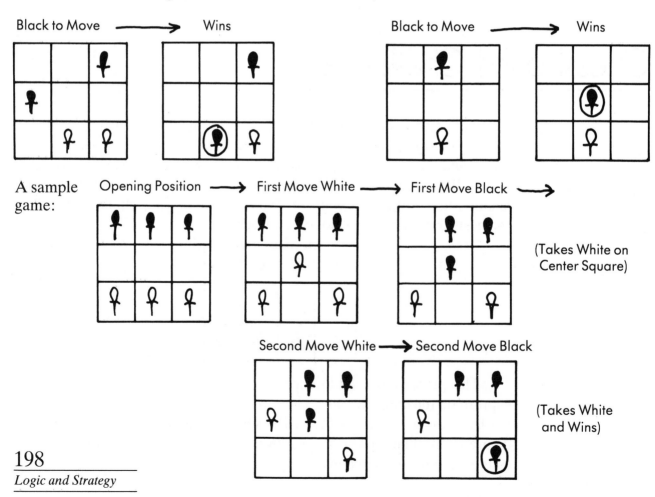

Here is an analysis of the best game strategy. It is in effect a mathematical proof of the fact that—no matter how the first player plays the game—if the second player makes the best possible moves, he or she will always win. Proofs about game strategies use the same structures and logical arguments that mathematical proofs use. Because of this, studying the ways games work is a good way to hone the habit of mathematical thinking.

Let's look at the initial position of the pieces:

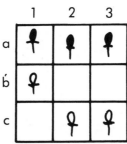

With White going first, there are three possible first moves: W1 → b1, or W2 → b2, or W3 → b3.*

It is not really necessary to consider all three moves, since the W1 and W3 moves are mirror images of each other, and any argument that can be made about moves of W1 and responses to that move can also be made about W3.

Only two first moves need be considered: W1 → b1; W2 → b2.

Take the first case: W1 → b1

What is Black's best move? Black can only make three replies:

$$BL2 \rightarrow b1(X)$$
$$BL2 \rightarrow b2$$
$$BL3 \rightarrow b3$$

Suppose Black chooses the third possibility and moves BL3 → b3. Then white moves W1 → a2(X) and wins.

*(X) after a move indicates a capture. W1 → b2(X) means a capture is made on White's move.

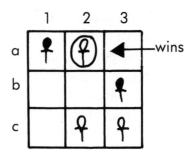

Clearly Black must choose another move. How about BL2 → b1(X)?

Now White has to take BL2 (which is on b1), or Black will move to c1 and win the game (or take W2 and move to c2 and also win).

After White takes BL2, the board looks like this:

Black has only one move, BL3 → b3, which is a winning move, since White is then pinned down and cannot make another move.

There is only one other possibility for Black's first move in reply to White's first move: BL2 → b2. The board would then look like this:

White can then move W3 → b3 and, by pinning down Black, win—so this is a dumb move for Black to make.

To summarize the argument, if White makes a first move W1 → b1, there are three possible responses yielding the following results:

$$W1 \to b1 \begin{cases} BL2 \to b1(X) \text{ wins} \\ BL2 \to b2 \text{ loses} \\ BL3 \to b3 \text{ loses} \end{cases}$$

Black has three responses to White's move W1 → b1, two of which provide losses and one of which guarantees a win, if Black (the second player to move) plays intelligently. So far, there are good reasons to want to be the second to move in this game.

There is only one opening move left to analyze, W2 → b2:

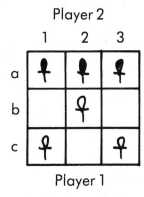

The white piece at b2 has to be taken by BL1 or BL3. If not, after Black's move (say, BL3 → b3), White would be able to capture and win: W2 → a1(X). Let's suppose BL1 → b2(X). Then the board looks like this:

At this point there are a number of possible moves for White to make. Let's consider first the moves of the piece at c3. This piece (W3) can move forward to b3. However, Black would reply by BL1 → c2 and win. The move left for W3 is to take the black piece at b2, leaving the board:

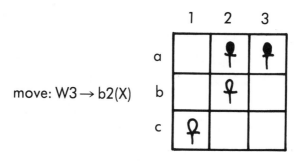

move: W3 → b2(X)

Black can then respond BL3 → b3, and after White's W1 → b1 (the only move possible for White at this point), move BL3 → c3 and win.

So far, there is no way that Black (the second person to play) can lose if he or she plays intelligently. Now let's consider a final possibility.

When the board is at this position:

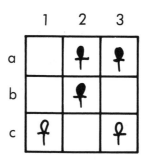

Player 1 can move the piece at c1 instead of the piece at c3 (whose moves were just analyzed). The piece at c1 (designated as W1) can move forward to b1. In that case, Black moves BL1 (on square b2) → c2 and wins.

W1 has one other move: W1 → b2(X). However, then the move BL3 → b3 is also a win, since White cannot move:

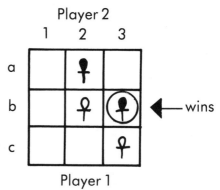

The conclusion of the analysis is that—no matter how well the first player plays this game—if the second player makes the best moves available, the second player will always win.

Here's another way to use a chesslike game to develop thinking skills.

The game is Minimal Chess. It involves the smallest board and game using all the pieces and rules of chess—not a particularly good way to introduce the game of chess (the whole board seems better), but a good way to get people who know the moves and rules to think strategically. It takes a 5-by-5 board. Each side has five pawns, and one each of king, queen, bishop, knight, and rook.

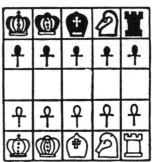

Chess- and checkerboards make wonderful palettes for the puzzler and the puzzle maker. Here are a number of classical chessboard challenges. After you've tried a few, create your own puzzles. All you need is a chess set, a board, a little ingenuity, and a lot of experimentation.

The Minimal Knights' Problem

What is the smallest number of knights that can be placed on a square board so that all unoccupied cells are under attack by at least one knight? Here are the solutions for three-sided to eight-sided boards.

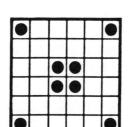

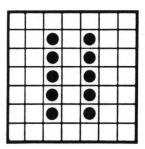

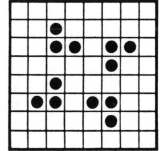

What is the largest number of knights that can be placed on a board so that no two attack each other?

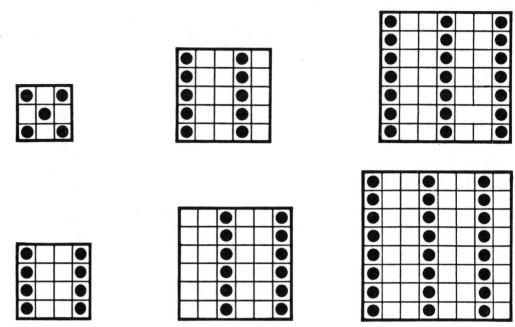

Here's a more complicated mathematical example of a chessboard problem, along with the analysis of the problem. It is taken from Fred Schuh's *Master Book of Mathematical Recreations,* which is a classic in the field and an invaluable resource for anyone interested in approaching mathematics through gaming.

Knight on the Chessboard

Knight's tour: As you know, the knight moves two squares horizontally and one square vertically, or one square horizontally and two squares vertically. By a closed knight's tour, we mean a broken line, formed by knight's moves, that ends at the starting point and that does not enter any square more than once. The problem is to divide the sixty-four squares of the chessboard into a number of closed tours that have no square in common, and in particular to pass through the sixty-four squares in one closed tour. It is not too difficult to find such a closed tour. Essentially different solutions exist in large number, and it would be extremely laborious to find them all.

Instead of the entire chessboard, we can take some set of the squares of this board and require a division of these squares into closed tours. Since the knight jumps from a white square to a black square, or vice versa, a closed knight's tour must contain an equal number of white and black squares. Hence, a given set of squares certainly cannot be divided into closed tours (or be passed through by one tour) when the numbers of white and black squares are different (in particular, this shows that the number of squares has to be even). This does not mean, however, that a division into closed tours is always possible when there are as many white squares as black.

Simple examples of closed knight's tours: In a 3-by-4 rectangle (that is, a rectangle divided into 3 × 4 squares), or in a 4-by-4 or a 4-by-5 rectangle, a division into closed tours is possible in one way only (see figure 1).

The centers of the squares are represented by dots. In the first diagram we obtain two closed tours of six moves each, in the second diagram four tours of four moves each, and in the third diagram two tours of ten moves each. Drawing the tours is extremely simple. You start in the four corners; from each of the corners, the two moves can be made in one way only. Then you turn your attention to other dots from which no move has yet been made and from which moves can be made to two dots only (naturally, you cannot move to a dot already used for two moves). With a 3-by-6 rectangle, this leads you to an impasse, so these eighteen squares cannot be divided into closed knight's tours.

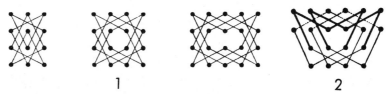

1
2

The next case, with twenty dots (or squares), is slightly more complicated. We start with the moves, indicated by heavy lines in Figure 2, from four dots of the uppermost row. After that, we can draw the thin lines from the dots of the bottom row; from this the dotted moves follow. We obtain two closed tours of ten moves each.

The figures described are all symmetrical and produce no other solutions by reflection.

Other closed knight's tours: In the case of a 3-by-8 rectangle, you have to distinguish between several cases after having drawn the sixteen moves that are indicated by heavy lines in the diagrams of figure 3. The distinction is made by the thin lines; the dotted lines are drawn last. The division into cases has been arranged in such a way that figures which arise from each other by rotation or reflection appear only once.* In the first diagram, we have one tour of eight moves, two tours of six moves each, and one tour of four moves. In the third diagram, we have four tours of six

---

*In all of these examples, solutions are considered identical if you rotate the board 90, 180, or 270 degrees without changing the positions of the lines, points, or pieces. Solutions are also considered identical to their reflected mirror images.

moves each, while in each of the three diagrams we have one tour of eighteen moves and one tour of six moves.

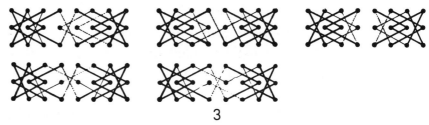

3

The case of a 3-by-10 rectangle requires more work. A restriction to pass through the thirty squares in one closed tour makes for a considerable simplification in the distinction of different cases (again indicated by thinly drawn lines in figure 4).

You can divide the thirty squares into more than one closed tour in seven essentially different ways: in two ways by tours of twenty, six, and four moves; in two ways by tours of eighteen, eight, and four moves; in two ways by two tours of eight, one of six, and two of four moves; and in one way by one tour of ten, two of six, and two of four moves. We leave it to the reader to draw these closed knight's tours in the various cases.

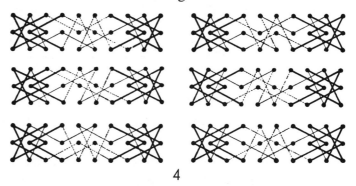

4

Weak Whites

Can you place the sixteen white pieces on a chessboard so that each piece protects only one other piece? Here's one solution. Try to find others.

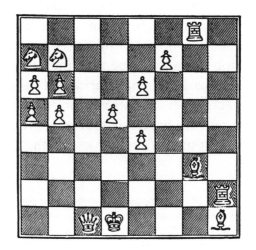

Four in Line

Below we have a board of thirty-six squares, and four counters are so placed in a straight line that every square of the board is in line horizontally, vertically, or diagonally with at least one counter. In other words, if you regard them as chess queens, every square on the board is attacked by at least one queen. The puzzle is to find in how many different ways the four counters may be placed in a straight line so that every square shall thus be in line with a counter.

Every arrangement in which the counters occupy a different set of four squares is a different arrangement. Thus, in the case of the example given, they can be moved to the next column to the right with equal effect, or they may be transferred to either of the two central rows of the board. This arrangement, therefore, produces four solutions by reversals or reflections of the board.

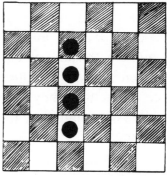

Solution:

There are nine fundamentally different arrangements, as shown below, A being the arrangement given as an example. Of these, D, E, and I each give eight solutions, counting reversals and reflections, and the others give only four solutions each. There are, therefore, in all, forty-eight different ways in which the four counters may be placed on the board so that every square is in line with at least one counter.

A   B   C

D   E   F

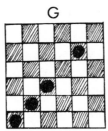
G

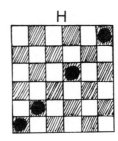
H

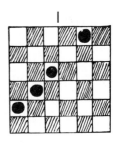
I

Some Games from Martin's Garden

Martin Gardner, in his "Mathematical Recreations" column in *Scientific American* and his more than thirty books, has introduced many strategy games developed by mathematicians to a wider audience. Here is a sampler, along with some of his comments on how strategies for winning them have been analyzed. Notice that all of the games I've chosen have no chance elements. They don't use dice, spinners, or lotteries. The outcomes are determined by the structure of the rules and the intelligence of the players.

One-Symbol Tic-Tac-Toe

You have a row of cells:

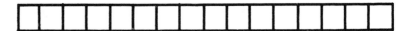

Players take turns by using the *same* mark, say an X, and trying to get three X's in a row. If the length of the field is odd, the first player can win by taking the center cell and then playing symmetrically until he sees a chance to win. But if the length is *even,* the game is unsolved! Winners are known only for small boards, but there is *no* sign of a general strategy.

Ulam's Triplet Game

The players take turns placing single counters until one player wins by getting three-in-a-row horizontally, vertically, or diagonally. The illustration shows a position on the order-6 board for which the next player must lose. Why?

Colin Vout's Dodgem

In 1972, when Colin Vout was a mathematics student at the University of Cambridge, he invented a fascinating counter game that he calls Dodgem because it is so often necessary for a piece to dodge around enemy pieces. It is playable on a checkerboard of any size. Even the game on a 3-by-3 board is complicated enough to be interesting.

Two black counters and two white ones are initially placed as shown in the upper illustration below. Black sits on the south side of the board and White sits on the west. The players alternately move a counter one space forward or to their left or right, unless it is blocked by another counter of either color or by an edge of the board. Each player's goal is to move all his pieces off the far side of the board. In other words, Black moves in a straight line north, west, or east and attempts to move both of his pieces off the north side of the board. White moves east, north, or

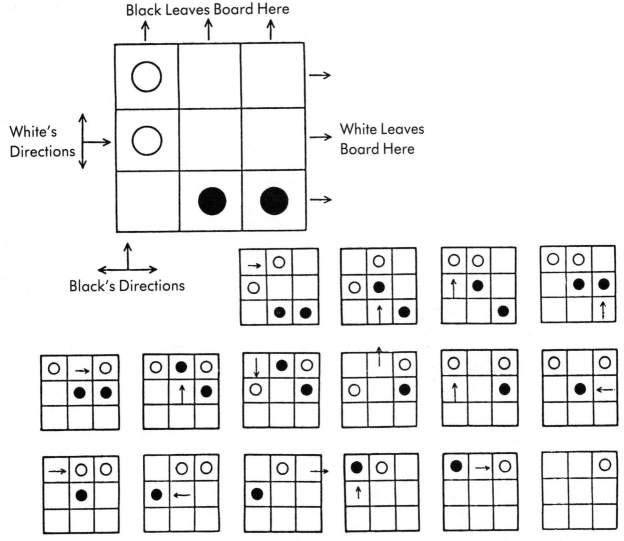

A Dodgem Game Won by Black

*Some Games from
Martin's Garden*

south and tries to move his pieces off the east side of the board.

There are no captures. A player must always leave his opponent a legal move or else forfeit the game. The first to get all his pieces off the board wins. The lower illustration shows a typical game won by Black.

Vout assures us that the first player always wins on the 3-by-3 board, but evidently no games on larger boards have yet been solved. On a board of side n, each player has $n - 1$ pieces placed on the west and south edges, with the southwest corner space vacant. Played with seven checkers or pawns of one color and seven of another color on the standard 8-by-8 checkerboard or chessboard, it is a most enjoyable game.

❊ Postscript ❊

Lewis Carroll got me thinking about puzzlements. I had never heard the word until I came upon this quotation in one of his letters: "A state of puzzlement is good for the young as it leads to a spirit of enquiry." The concept of "a state of puzzlement" is what fascinated me. It implied a condition of life, a continuous quest to understand things in the world and the mind, and, most importantly, a delight in the pleasures that thinking can provide.

What I have tried to do in this book is convey some of the pleasures that thinking mathematically can provide in those moments we can steal from the usual, everyday demands upon us to make things useful and profitable.

And I discovered—in Lewis Carroll once again—advice on how to go about indulging in mathematical pleasure. I can think of no better way to end this book than to quote his advice to someone who was teaching herself mathematics for the joy of it:

> I think I shall be of . . . use to you by giving a few hints as to mathematical study generally. And the first shall be "When you have made a thorough, and reasonably long effort, to understand a thing, and still feel puzzled by it, *stop*. You will only hurt yourself by going on. Put it aside till the next morning: and if *then* you can't make it out, and have no one to explain it to you, put it aside entirely, and go back to that part of the subject which you *do* understand." When I was reading Mathematics for University honours, I would sometimes, after working a week or two at some new book, and mastering 10 or 20 pages, get into a hopeless muddle, and find it just as bad the next morning. My rule was *to begin the book again*. And perhaps in another fortnight I had come to the old difficulty with impetus enough to get over it. Or perhaps not. I have several books that I have begun over and over again.
>
> My second hint shall be—"Never leave an unsolved difficulty *behind*." I mean, don't go any further in that book, till the difficulty is conquered. In this point, Mathematics differs entirely from most other subjects. Suppose you are reading an Italian book, and come to a hopelessly obscure sentence. Don't waste too much time on it. Skip it, and go on. You will do very well without it. But if you skip a *mathematical* difficulty, it is sure to crop up again: you will find some other proof depending on it, and you will only get deeper and deeper into the mud.
>
> My third hint is "only go on working so long as the brain is *quite* clear."

The moment you feel the ideas getting confused, leave off and rest, or your penalty will be that you will never learn Mathematics *at all!* Believe me
Your sincere friend (without the least idea who you are!),
Lewis Carroll*

The Letters of Lewis Carroll, edited by Morton N. Cohen with the assistance of Roger Lancelyn Green (New York: Oxford University Press, 1979), 558–59.

✳ Recommended Reading ✳

There are a number of books currently in print that deal in greater detail with the topics in this book. I have deliberately kept the present list small. Once you plunge into the books, you'll be led to many other works in the field of mathematical recreations. They all have bibliographies, and mathematical recreationists are notoriously kind in giving each other credit and recommending each other's work.

The best way to begin is to pick up one or two books by Martin Gardner. His work is clear, beautifully written, and accessible. It is fun. It is also generous, and one always takes away ideas and challenges and references from a session with Martin. Here are some of his books (he has written over thirty):

Mathematical Puzzles and Diversions (New York: Simon and Schuster, 1961)

Martin Gardner's New Mathematical Diversions from Scientific American (Chicago: University of Chicago Press, 1984)

Mathematical Carnival (New York: Alfred A. Knopf, 1975)

Mathematical Circus (New York: Random House, 1981)

Martin Gardner's Sixth Book of Mathematical Diversions from Scientific American (Chicago: University of Chicago Press, 1984)

Another way to warm yourself up to play with mathematics is to read Lewis Carroll. Modern Library has published an inexpensive edition of *The Complete Works of Lewis Carroll,* which includes hundreds of puzzles and challenges as well as *Alice's Adventures in Wonderland* and *Through the Looking Glass.*

PART 1: PATTERNS ON THE PLANE

Edwin A. Abbott's *Flatland: A Romance of Many Dimensions* (5th rev. ed.; New York: Barnes and Noble, 1983) is an early classic of life within a plane that, along with A. K. Dewdney's *Planiverse: Computer Contact with a Two-Dimensional World* (New York: Poseidon Press, 1984), will challenge and delight your imagination as they draw you into complex two-dimensional worlds. After an excursion in two dimensions, you might want to challenge yourself to play in four-dimensional space. If so, *The Fourth Dimension: Toward a Geometry of Higher Reality,* by Rudy Rucker (Boston: Houghton Mifflin, 1984), is a wonderful guidebook.

Peter S. Stevens' *Handbook of Regular Patterns: An Introduction to*

Symmetry in Two Dimensions (Cambridge, Mass.: MIT Press, 1981) is a beautiful book on how to produce patterns ranging from simple repeats to complex tessellations and tilings. It is the most useful book on design on the plane I have ever encountered.

Another book worth reading is Douglas Hofstadter's *Gödel, Escher, Bach: An Eternal Golden Braid* (New York: Basic Books, 1979).

PART 2: NUMBER PATTERNS

There are dozens of books that will keep you busy with number challenges—simple, complex, and impossible. Three of my favorites are:

Mathematic Diversions, by J. A. Hunter and Joseph S. Madachy (New York: Dover, 1975)

Mathematics on Vacation, by Joseph S. Madachy (New York: Scribner's, 1966)

The Master Book of Mathematical Recreations, by Fred Schuh (New York: Dover, 1968).

If you become obsessed with number diversions (and many of the other topics in this book), subscribe to the *Journal of Recreational Mathematics* (Baywood Publishing Company, 120 Marine Street, Box D, Farmingdale, N.Y. 11735).

PART 3: KNOTS, MAPS, AND CONNECTIONS

Hugo Steinhaus' *Mathematical Snapshots* (3d ed.; New York: Oxford University Press, 1969) is a beautifully illustrated, extremely challenging series of puzzlements. It covers a wide range of mathematical topics, some of which are difficult. It is especially good on knots, maps, and connections. For a beginning introduction to these subjects, try Mitch Struble, *Stretching a Point* (Philadelphia: Westminster Press, 1971).

A classic in knotting and all types of gaming is Elwyn R. Berlekamp, John Conway, and Richard K. Guy, *Winning Ways for Your Mathematical Plays* (Orlando, Fla.: Academic Press, 1982). This beautifully written, playful, and brightly illustrated book is very rich and in parts extremely difficult. There are two volumes (published separately): *Games in General* and *Games in Particular.* I suggest you plunge into the ingenious games and analyses in volume 2 first and then take a pass at the more theoretical volume 1.

PART 4: LOGIC AND STRATEGY

Raymond Smullyan's *What Is the Name of This Book?: The Riddle of Dracula and Other Logical Puzzles* (Englewood Cliffs, N.J.: Prentice-Hall, 1978) and *The Chess Mysteries of Sherlock Holmes* (New York: Alfred A. Knopf, 1979) should keep you busy for a while and perhaps cause you a headache or two. They are fun and full courses in logic as well.

Finally, I would like to recommend Claudia Zaslavsky's *Africa Counts: Number and Pattern in African Culture* (Boston: Prindle, Weber, and Schmidt, 1973), which is a rich survey of mathematics and mathematical games throughout the African continent. It is the only introduction to African mathematical thinking I have encountered.

❧ Acknowledgments ❧

Pages 11 bottom, 12 top, 13 middle, 18 top, 19 bottom, 20 bottom, 21 all, 22 top, 23 bottom–25 top, 71 bottom–72 top, from *Handbook of Regular Patterns* by Peter S. Stevens. Copyright © 1980, 1981 MIT Press, Cambridge, Mass. Reprinted by permission of the publisher.

Pages 12 bottom, 15 lower right corner by Varvara Stepanova from *Art into Production: Soviet Textiles, Fashion and Ceramics 1917–1935*. Used by permission of Alexander Lavrentev Rodchenko.

Page 13 top, 15 large pattern lower left and "ship" pattern, page 19 middle from *Soviet Textile Design of the Revolutionary Period* by I. Yasinskaya. Published by Idea Books, Milano, and used by permission of the publisher.

Page 22 lower part, 23 top, 24 top (Figures 3 and 4), 71 (Figure 3) are all © M. C. Escher Heirs, c/o Cordon Art, Baarn, Holland. Used by permission of Cordon Art.

Pages 38–40, 103–106, 125–128 top, from *Sources of Mathematical Discovery* by Lorraine Mottershead. Co-published by Basil Blackwell, England, and Jacaranda Wiley, Australia, and used with their permission.

Pages 44–45, 84, 88–91, 100–102 top from Vol. 11, No. 3, 1978–79; Vol. 11, No. 4, 1978–79; Vol. 15, No. 2, 1982–83; Vol. 12, No. 2, 1979–80, Vol. 13, No. 2, 1980–81 of *Journal of Recreational Mathematics*. Used by permission of Baywood Publishing Company, Incorporated.

Pages 47–48, 50 (bottom illustration), 51 (top illustration), 52–54 from *Planiverse* by Alexander K. Dewdney. Copyright © 1984 by Alexander K. Dewdney. Reprinted by permission of Poseidon Press, a division of Simon & Schuster, Inc., McClelland & Stewart Ltd., and Pan Books Ltd.

Pages 58–61, 146, 206 bottom–208 top from *Henry Ernest Dudeney: 536 Puzzles and Curious Problems* edited by Martin Gardner. Used by permission of Martin Gardner.

Pages 62–65 edited from work by Claudia Zaslavsky and used with her permission.

Pages 65–71 top from Nuffield Mathematics Project Modules (1973) *Symmetry* by Chambers/Murray/Wiley. Used by permission of Nuffield-Chelsea Curriculum Trust.

Pages 72–73, 74, 75 from *The Fractal Geometry of Nature* by Benoit Mandelbrot. Copyright © 1982. Used by permission of the author.

Pages 76, 77, 204–206 from *Master Book of Mathematical Recreations* by Fred Schuh. Published by Dover Publications, Inc., and used with their permission.

Page 115 from pages 586–587 of *Funk and Wagnalls Standard Dictionary of Folklore, Mythology and Legend* edited by Maria Leach and Jerome Fried. Copyright 1949, 1950, © 1972 by Harper & Row, Publishers, Inc. Reprinted by permission of Harper & Row, Publishers, Inc.

Pages 120–121 top from *Tricks and Amusements with Coins, Cards, String, Paper and Matches* by R. M. Abraham. Published by Dover Publications, Inc., and used with their permission.

Pages 122–123 top from *Celtic Art: The Methods of Constructions* by George Bain. By permission of Stuart Titles Ltd., 268 Bath Street, Glasgow, Great Britain.

Pages 123 bottom and 124 from pages 16 and 17 of *Paper Folding for the Mathematics Classroom* by Donavan A. Johnson. Published by the National Council of the Teachers of Mathematics and reprinted with their permission.

Page 128 (Möbius Hat) adapted from an article by Joan Ross which appeared in *Mathematics Teacher,* April 1985. Used by permission of Joan Ross.

Pages 130–131 (The Two-Color Theorem) from *Super Games* (original title *Geometrie als Spiel*) by Ivan Moscovich. Reprinted by permission of the publisher, Otto Maier Verlag GmbH.

Pages 132–135 from *Your Move* by David L. Silverman. Published by Dover Publications, Inc., and used with their permission.

Pages 135 bottom–138 from *Mathematics and the Imagination* by Edward Kasner and James Newman. Copyright 1940 by Edward Kasner and James Newman, renewed © 1967 by Ruth G. Newman. Reprinted by permission of Simon & Schuster, Inc.

Pages 143 bottom–145, 182–183 from *Gamesmag* (April 1977): Vol. 2, No. 3; (March 1976): Vol. 1, No. 4; (December 1976): Vol. 1, No. 9 and from an unpublished manuscript. By permission of the author, Claudia Zaslavsky.

Pages 147–152 from *Mathematical Carnival* by Martin Gardner. Copyright © 1965, 1966, 1967, 1968, 1975 by Martin Gardner. Reprinted by permission of Alfred A. Knopf, Inc. By permission also of George Allen & Unwin Ltd.

Pages 156–163 from *Winning Ways for Your Mathematical Plays,* Volume 2: *Games in Particular* by Elwyn R. Berlekamp, John H. Conway, and Richard K. Guy. Copyright © 1982 by Academic Press Inc. (London) Ltd. Reprinted by permission of the publisher.

Pages 167–170 from *What Is the Name of This Book?* by Raymond Smullyan. Copyright © 1978 by Raymond M. Smullyan. Reprinted by permission of Simon & Schuster, Inc.

Pages 171 bottom–178 from "How to Solve Logic Problems" by Alan Duncum. Reprinted by permission from *Logic Problems Magazine,* British European Associated Publishers Limited.

Pages 179–181 from *Following Directions—B* by Anita Harnadek, published by Midwest Publications. Extensive research failed to locate the author and/or copyright holder of this work.

Pages 184–193 by Bernard DeKoven. Excerpted from *Playworks! Incorporated.* Used by permission of Bernard DeKoven.

Page 208 (One-Symbol Tic-Tac-Toe) by Martin Gardner and used by permission of the author.

Pages 208–210 (Ulam's Triplet Game and Colin Vout's Dodgem) from *Scientific American,* June 1975. They appeared in "Martin's Garden" by Martin Gardner. Copyright © 1975 by Scientific American, Inc. All rights reserved. Used by permission.

✄ Index ✄